How to Master the Bible

Rev. Martin Anstey

How to Master the Bible

Contact:
BibliotechPress@gmail.com

ISBN: 978-1-61895-207-3

Contents

Chapter 1
How to Understand the Bible

THE Bible is a plain, honest, straightforward, simple Book. It is easy to read and easy to understand. It needs no learned introduction, no expert scholarship to enable us to grasp its meaning. It was written for the people and it has not missed its mark. It is a people's Book; therefore a classic. It is an exhaustive, work; therefore a standard. It readily discloses its secret to men of pure heart and simple faith, whether college-trained or unacquainted with the learning of the schools. The primary requisite of the Bible student is a sincere desire to know the will of God in order that he may do it. The Bible is a revelation of the will of God. Its primary appeal is to the will of man. It was written to be obeyed. Hence the primary qualification demanded in the reader is not scholarship but surrender, not expert knowledge but willingness to be led by the Spirit of God. Simple piety will feed on the inner spiritual kernel of Scripture. Pride of intellect will break its teeth upon its external literary shell.

It is not necessary to preface our study of the Bible with a course of Bible Introduction. The purpose for which the Bible was written, the purpose for which it ought to be read, may be accomplished without any knowledge of the conclusions of modern Biblical criticism as to the writers and the readers of the several books, the time when and the place where they were written, their simple or composite character, or the grounds on which they have been assigned a place in the sacred Canon. Bible Introduction may enhance our knowledge of the circumstances under which the books of the Bible were composed, but it is a poor substitute for the deeper and more exact knowledge of the message and content of the books themselves.

Bible Study is the study of the Bible not the study of problems relating to the composition of the Text and the transmission of the Canon.

The Bible is an open Book, not a cypher message the key to the interpretation of which is in the possession of the learned. It requires no preliminary course of study initiating us into the method of its composition and the mystery of its meaning. The essential content of the Bible, the facts recorded, the truths taught, and the precepts enjoined are within the compass of the most ordinary reader. The principal qualification for the right understanding of the Bible is a pure heart, a simple faith, and an obedient will. We must be in sympathy with the Divine aim and purpose of the Book which is to make unholy, men holy, and to make holy men holier still. We must be prepared to accept as authentic the things which it records as facts. We must be prepared to believe as true the interpretation which it gives of the real significance and meaning of those facts. And we must be prepared to obey the precepts which it enjoins as arising necessarily out of those facts and those truths.

The first necessity for the understanding of the Bible is the removal of all the embargoes which have been placed upon the operation of the Spirit of God in opening and illuminating the mind of the reader. Through the Word of God the Spirit of God awakens a clear conviction of the certainty of the facts recorded, the truth of the interpretations placed upon those facts, and the imperative necessity of obeying the will of God as made known in and through them.

The Bible is pre-eminently a manual of life and conduct for the layman. In the early days of the Christian Church, as also at the time of the Reformation, and again in the century following the great Evangelical Revival ushered in by the preaching of Whitefield and Wesley, the real meaning, the true purport, and the actual content of the Bible were well understood. The Bible was an open Book, " understanded of the people." Lay-preachers abounded. The Gospel message was grasped by all and proclaimed by all. The assumption of the incapacity of the unlettered layman to ascertain the true meaning of the Word of God must be resisted at all costs. It is made by the craft of the critic no less than by the craft of the Romish priest. It must be disallowed both in the interest of the truth itself, and also in the interest of the right of the laity to assist in the proclamation of the truth, without having to undergo a preliminary course of instruction in the very questionable results of modern Biblical Criticism.

The true key to the understanding of the Word of God is the sincere desire to ascertain just exactly what the Spirit of God in the sacred writers intended to convey. We must not take their words and read into them a meaning of our own.. We must receive the Word whether it accords with our preconceptions or contradicts them. We must interpret literally everything that was meant to be interpreted literally, and we must interpret figuratively everything that was meant to be interpreted figuratively.

Thus the early chapters of Genesis are not sacred myths but historic facts. The book of Jonah is not an allegory but the record of a historic event. The Son of Solomon is an inspired idyll to be interpreted not literally as if it were a common secular love song, and not allegorically as if it meant something altogether different from that which it says, but typically, as setting forth, under the type of the transcendent experiences of human life and human love, the still deeper mysteries of the union of the soul and its Saviour, of Christ and His Church. `

The allegorical method of Origin and Christian fathers of Alexandria, which empties the records of the Old Testament of their content of historical reality, and the hypothetical method of modern Biblical Criticism, which accounts for the whole content of Scripture upon naturalistic principles, and leaves no room for the transcendent operation of the Spirit of God, are both alike to be rejected as wholly incompatible with the plain declarations of the Word of God itself, , and a virtual denial of its claim to be a supernatural and a real revelation of the mind and will of God to men.

The Bible will never be understood until it is received for what in truth it is-a transcript from real life. The Bible is always true to itself. There are no real discrepancies and no real contradictions in it, though it can easily be so misinterpreted that the critic may be able to get many discrepancies and contradictions out of it. The Bible is always true to life. There are no contradictions between the facts stated in Scripture and the facts which have been ascertained and brought to light in any department of modern literary and scientific research. Astronomy, geology, archaeology, comparative religion, and Biblical Criticism in all its branches, have yielded no single instance of inaccuracy or unreliability in the written Word of God.

It is necessary to state the case thus strongly in view of the widely prevalent assumption that in some of these respects the accuracy and the authority of the Bible have been discredited. But whatever may be the learning and the scholarship of those who deny the authenticity and the harmony of the Biblical records, and however frequently the assertion of inaccuracy and unreliability may be made, the refutation of the charge is complete, and the Bible stands today, as it ever has stood, a well-spring of Divine truth, in every detail clear and pure and undefiled.

For an illustration of the truth of this statement the reader is referred to the author's "Romance of Bible Chronology," where in spite of the assertion of all manner of chronological discrepancies in the Text of the Old Testament, it is conclusively proved that every date given in the Old Testament is in perfect accord with every other date given therein, and also with every date obtained from contemporary monuments, such as the cuneiform inscriptions in the British Museum. The Biblical narrative is thus seen to be both self-consistent and self-sufficient, and also in perfect accord with all the facts that , have been brought to light by modern discovery and recent research. A similarly detailed study of any other class of alleged discrepancies will establish in like manner the entire accuracy and the complete authenticity of the Biblical records.

The Bible will never disclose its meaning to the man who approaches it in a spirit of doubt, who turns its facts into fables, its certificates of authenticity into late forgeries, and its theophanies into the subtle workings of the subliminal consciousness of men. The Bible must be treated with reverence as well as with intelligence. Its solemn testimonies must be accepted in good faith as trustworthy communication of the mind and will of God to men. The Bible student must be a man of prayer, in living communion with the living God, who utters His voice in the living soul. As the eyes fall upon the printed page the Spirit of God defines and perpetuates for all time the exact content and the true meaning of the Eternal Word. Divine power resides in the Word. It inheres in every translation of the Word. It penetrates the heart, illuminates the understanding, and invigorates the will. Every sympathetic and sincere soul may understand, if he is willing to obey, the holy will of God made known in His Holy Word.

Chapter 2
How to Enjoy the Bible

Hunger is the best sauce. The Bible is the meeting point of many interests, intellectual, scientific, antiquarian, emotional, artistic, - literary, moral, and spiritual. It touches us on every side. It sounds the deepest depths of human sorrow. It lifts us up to the noblest heights of human exaltation. But the leading interest of the Book is spiritual. It is not easy to enlist the interest and the sympathy of the man who has no appetite for the things of God in a course of Bible Study.

The chief cause of the neglect of Bible Study in the present day is the surrender of the soul to the prevailing attractions of material interests and worldly ambitions. If a man is not interested in spiritual things, if he does not know and does not want to know what he must do in order to become holy and acceptable to God, it will be difficult to convince him of the incomparable fascination and the supreme joy of true Bible Study. But given a healthy appetite and a wholesome taste for the things that conduce to purity and goodness and real greatness of soul, the Bible is an unfailing source of perpetual delight.

The intellectual or scientific interest of the Bible is superior to that of any other similar pursuit. Its antiquarian interest appeals to all who are concerned with the records of the past in a way that cannot be paralleled by the appeal of the classics, or that of the ancient literary monuments of the East. The study of the Bible leads to the discovery of ever-deepening wonders and undreamed-of glories, which startle the soul and plunge it into ecstasies of delight, exceeding in intensity and power the rapture experienced by the man of science - when some new truth flashes upon his mind, with the revelation of hidden harmonies, the solution of baffling problems, and the proof of long-cherished hypotheses. The solution of difficulties, the clearing up of discrepancies, the reconciliation of apparent contradictions, and the attainment of a clear perception of the perfect harmony which penetrates into the last detail and permeates and pervades the entire structure of Holy Scripture, is a source of unfailing intellectual interest. The Bible is a world in itself, and its hidden harmonies monies are as simple and as perfect, as complete and as profound, as those which underlie the unity of the world, which forms the subject of the investigation of the scientist and the philosopher.

The artistic or emotional interest of the Bible is not less but greater than that of any other literary work. No one can read the book of Ruth, the history of Joseph, or the dramatic episode of the book of Esther without being deeply touched, sometimes even . to tears; by the appeal which these narratives make to our affections and our sympathies ; whilst the book of Daniel, read, accepted, and believed in as the true history which it is, cannot fail to arouse the deepest feelings of admiration for the courage, the heroism, and the faith in God which the history portrays, and the triumphant conclusion to which it eventually attains. For pure artistic skill and literary power the narrative portions of Scripture are without a peer in the literature of all ages. They make the Bible the most inter esting Book in the whole world.

The moral interest of the Bible touches the deeps of childhood, of maturity, and of old age. It kindles in childhood a passionate desire to live a worthier, a nobler, and a better life ; it fires the enthusiasm of youth with the same strenuous purpose ; and it sustains the moral elevation of those whose sun is westering and soon to sink into the rest of eventide.

But the supreme interest of the Bible is the interest of the spirit-the interest of holiness,and the supernatural craving for a closer walk with God. In the rich and deep and tranquil satisfaction which it affords to the longing of the soul for perfect union with God, the Bible stands alone. It exhibits the perfect pattern of lowliness, the true type of self-sacrifice, the authentic model of godly fear. The life of the spirit is nourished, expanded, and perfected in feeding upon the Word. The soul is sustained in sorrow, the will is strengthened in conflict, the heart is purified from sin, the intellect is clarified and freed from doubt, the character is established in righteousness and truth, and the new nature is 'imparted to the child of God through the deeper study of the Word of God.

One of the surest methods of promoting the enjoyment of the Word of God is the habit of seeing the truth of each portion of Scripture in the light of the great central truth of the whole. We need to grasp the scope and purpose of the Bible as an organic whole to have a clear conception of the specific aim of each book it contains, and an equally vivid insight into its relation to the general aim of the whole Bible of which it forms an organic part. One of the chief sources of the supposed contradictions of Scripture is the practice of ignoring the relation of the various books to each other, to the testament to which they belong, and to the Bible as a whole. In this matter the golden rule is "Distinguish the dispensations and the difficulties will disappear." One of the chief delights of Bible Study is the growing perception with increasing study of the perfect harmony which obtains between the older revelation and the new, the earlier books and the later, regard being had to the dispensation to which each portion of Scripture belongs.

The complete mastery of the truths revealed in Holy Scripture, and the clear perception of their inner harmony, can only be obtained by long and patient investigation, reflection, and research ; but those who are willing to pay the price will be rewarded by the exhilarating sense of power which invariably accompanies persevering effort in the search for truth. A comprehensive grasp of the aim and purpose, the scope and content of the Bible, invests with deep and living interest the study of each individual book.

The habit of confining one's attention to the study of selected portions viewed by themselves apart from their relation to the context in which they are found, is in some degree responsible for the lack of interest which many Christians experience when the Bible is read in this way. It is necessary to survey the whole field in a systematic, consecutive, comprehensive way, if the interest of Bible Study is to be deepened and maintained.

The joy of Bible Study can only be experienced by those who obey its precepts and live the life which it enjoins and inspires. The Bible student must abandon all hypocrisy, all malice, all covetousness, and all indolence. He must forsake the sins which the Bible rebukes ; otherwise he will be unable to appreciate its noble counsels and its high commands, interest in the pursuit of the truth will decline, and eventually the study of the Word will be neglected and forsaken. Sin soon separates from the Bible those whom the Bible does not separate from sin.

Chapter 3
How to Authenticate the Bible

THE Bible is a living unity, an organic whole, it whose limits can never be disturbed by addition, alteration or withdrawal. It is a complete, a final, and an exhaustive revelation of the will of God to men.

The preservation of the correct Text and the transmission of the exact content of the Bible are not the work of mere human tradition. They are the outcome of the ever-watchful activity of Divine providence. The Church is not the creator but the custodian of the Canon, or list of books which constitute the Word of God.

The word "Canon" means a rod, a rule, a standard, an authority. As applied to the books of the Old and New Testament, it indicates that these writings and these alone constitute an exhaustive and an authoritative expression of the mind of God, an objective standard or rule of faith, and a final court of appeal, valid for all time in all matters pertaining to life and salvation. The word "Canon," as applied to the books of the Bible, indicates that these books are to be clearly distinguished and definitely marked off from all other literature as being of Divine origin and possessing Divine authority. They embody a divinely given standard, or rule of faith and practice, for all generations and for all mankind.

The Old Testament is a Divine revelation made by duly authorised and amply accredited messengers, chosen by God Himself and adequately furnished for this purpose. It was written down between the age of Moses and the age of Ezra and Malachi, a period of a, little over a thousand years. The authority of the various books of the Old Testament was not gradually acquired by them, but belonged to them from the very first. The written words of Moses and the prophets, like their spoken words, were immediately recognised as of Divine authority. They were not regarded as of Divine authority because they were found in the Canon, but they were placed in the Canon because they were immediately perceived by inspired men of God to be of Divine origin and authority. Their admission to the Canon was not due to their antiquity or to the fact that they were written in the sacred Hebrew language, but to the recognition of the truthfulness of their claim to be a direct and an authoritative revelation of the divinely communicated will of God.

8

Their Divine authority was imparted with and inherent in the words themselves, not subsequently added to them by a process of canonisation.

Moses and the prophets were invested with Divine authority. They were the messengers of Jehovah and they spoke in His name, so that the words they uttered were not of their own origination. That is the meaning of the words :" No prophecy of the Scripture is of any private interpretation " (2 Peter 1: 20). The prophecy is not of human origination.. It is the Word of the the Lord. It is "the law of God." The Word of the Lord was of the same binding authority,whether written or spoken. It was sacred and inviolable from the very first. Hence each book in the Bible has its own independent authority, which it derives directly from God, and not from the Church or council which, pronounces judgment on its claim to be an expression of His mind and will.

The exact definition of the true content of the Canon of the Old Testament was guaranteed by living prophets until the age of Ezra ; and Malachi, when the spirit of prophecy was withdrawn, the age of inspiration ceased, and the Canon of the Old Testament was closed. Proverbs 30:6, and Deuteronomy 4:2 and 10:32 define the character and fix the limits of the Canon of the Old Testament, as Revelation 22: 18,19 fixes the limit and closes the Canon of the New.

" Add thou not unto His words lest He reprove thee and thou be found a liar." Ye shall not add unto the word which I command you, neither shall ye diminish ought from it." "What thing soever I command you, observe and do it : thou shalt not add thereto, nor diminish from it." " If any man shall add unto these things God shall add unto him the plagues that are written in this book: and if any man shall take away from the words of the book of this prophecy, God shall take away his part out of the book of life and out of the holy city and from the things which are written in this Book."

Uninterrupted testimony ascribes the completion of the Canon of the Old Testament to Ezra and the Great Synagogue, and from the age of Ezra to the present day, through the Targums, the Sopherim, the Talmud, the Mishna, the Gemara, the Massoretes, the Manuscripts, the printed Hebrew Bibles and the activities of the Christian Church, it has been guarded and preserved amid all the vicissitudes of time by the ever-watchful eye and the all-protecting hand of God.

The authority of the Old Testament is guaranteed by the writers of the New Testament. Every book in the Old Testament is either quoted or alluded to in the New Testament. The Bible as we hold it in our , hands today is identical with the Bible as it was held in the hands of our Lord and His Apostles. They regarded the Old Testament as of Divine origin, as given by Divine inspiration, as invested with Divine authority.

In like manner the books of the New Testament are given by the inspiration of God through the Apostles, who were chosen by our Lord for this very purpose, that they might be with Him, and receive His Spirit, and be instructed by the Holy Ghost, and then go forth and bear witness, by Spirit-taught word and inspired pen, of the " things which they had seen and heard."

The authentication of the Word of God is it the work of the ever-living Spirit of God. The truth of the Word is for ever guaranteed by -the immediate testimony of the Spirit of God.

The authentication of the Canon, or list of hooks contained in the Old and New Testament, must be supplemented by the authentication of the Text of these books. This is the task of Biblical Criticism, a work demanding not only some degree of learning and scholarship, but also some measure of acquaintance with the mind of the Spirit.

Biblical Criticism is divided into three branches: (1) Textual or Lower Criticism ;.(2) Documentary or Higher Criticism ; (3) Speculative or Historical Criticism. Of these the first alone has anything of value to offer to the Bible student, for both Higher Criticism and Historical Criticism deal with speculative problems which can never be answered. Both alike proceed from naturalistic premises ; both alike tend to throw doubt upon the Divine origin, inspiration, and authority of the Bible, and the historical character of the events which it records; and both alike lead to results which are incompatible with the direct testimony of Scripture concerning itself.

Textual Criticism is occupied with the determination of the Text of Scripture. It deals with the reproduction of the true and genuine original Text of the books of the Old and New Testament, and the elimination of the errors which have crept into certain manuscripts through the carelessness of copyists and other causes. The work of the textual critics has been worth doing and well done. The material at their disposal is singularly abundant, especially in the number of authoritative copies of the Text of the New Testament. The original autographs have all perished, but their exact content has been accurately preserved to us by an immense array of witnesses, compared with which the authorities for the text of classical works is insignificant. We have two hundred and fifty manuscripts of Horace, and similarly numerous copies of Virgil, but only one manuscript of so important a work as Tacitus' "Annals." For Caesar, Herodotus, and Thucydides, we have only late copies of the ninth, tenth, and eleventh centuries A.D. The manuscripts of the New Testament, on the other hand, date from as early as from the fourth to the ninth century, and of these we have no fewer than three thousand copies in existence today.

Textual Criticism is a judicial process directed, to the determination of the precise words used by the original writer. There are two schools of Textual Criticism, the traditional and- the critical. The net result of their labours has been to establish beyond all question the entire accuracy of the Text of the New Testament, which lies at the basis of our English translations. The Revised Version embodies the Text adopted by members of the critical school -Westcott and Hort, Sanday and other scholars. The Authorised Version embodies the Text favoured by members of the traditional school-Burgon, Scrivener, Miller and others. Both schools contain men of equal learning and equal scholarship ; but all the members of both schools are so far agreed as to the entire genuineness of the Text translated, that not one single doctrine, and not more than six or seven important passages, are affected by the differences between them. In the Revised Version, doubt is cast upon the sufficiency of the ancient manuscript authority for (1) the last twelve verses of Mark (Mark 16: 9-20); (2) the word from the Cross, " Father forgive them ; for they know not what they do" (Luke 23: 34) ; (3) the record of the strengthening angel and the bloody sweat (Luke 22: 43, 44) ; (4) the form of the angelic hymn, " Peace on earth, good will toward men" (A.V.), instead of "Peace on earth to men of good will" (R.V.) (Luke 2: 14) ; (5) the Doxology in the Lord's prayer (Matt.6: 13) ; (6) the words descriptive of the Son of Man, "which is in heaven " (John 3: 13) ; and - (7) the words "God was manifest in the flesh" (A.V.) (1 Tim.3:16). Anyone who will read the Appendix in Miller's " Guide to the Textual Criticism of the New Testament " will see how strong is the evidence for, and how gratuitous is the doubt cast upon, the genuineness and the sufficiency of the original manuscript authority for these passages.

The Higher Criticism deals with the more difficult problems of the authorship and date of the various books of the Bible, their simple or composite character, and their literary form. It is concerned with questions relating to the origin and structure of the documents containing the Text as it has been handed down to us. Here again differences of method determine the point of view, and divide Biblical scholars into two camps, each containing men of great eminence, equally learned, equally honest, equally well equipped and equally "modern." The critical school challenges the predictive element in prophecy, and assigns a purely human origin and an obsolescent authority to the whole Bible. Its conclusions are declared to be the "assured results " of an honest, candid, scholarly examination of the literary phenomena presented in Biblical literature, but they are really due to naturalistic presuppositions which determine the method and fix the reader's point of view. 'The conclusions of the critical school are incompatible with the truth of the testimony of the Spirit of God contained in Holy Scripture itself.

Historical Criticism is a further development of the principles of the Higher Criticism. It denies the historical character of the authentic records of the Old Testament, and deals with testimony of the Spirit through the reading of the Word. We affirm, with no less honesty and candour, with no less reason and understanding of the points at issue, and with no less devotion to the supremacy of the claims of truth than those who hold the contrary opinion, that Adam and Noah, Joseph and Jonah, David and Daniel, are not myths but men, and that an unprejudiced, scholarly estimate of all the evidence available for the solution of the doubts which the critics have raised in relation to this matter, will lead to the inevitable judicial conclusion that the theories of the critics are false, whilst the affirmations of the Bible are true. We give the message in full. It has already appeared in a number of religious periodicals, but it is quite worthy of reproduction here.

DR PARKER'S LAST MESSAGE CONCERNING THE BIBLE

We were brought up amongst simple, unsuspecting believers. They told us that the Bible was all true. They called it " The Holy Bible," and they held it to be such. They told us that Eden was a real place, with real trees and a real serpent. They told us that a four-branched river rolled through the sunny paradise ; we thought that Adam bathed in Hiddekel ; and that the gold that coloured the Pison stream was solid, and yellow, and marketable. We never doubted it. The place on the map was pointed out, with the assurance that if

Eden was not there it was thereabouts. Some people believe this still. Spurgeon believed it. In its highest, deepest, grandest meaning, I myself believe it.

Our mothers are responsible for a good deal. They were not literal grammarians, but they were gigantic believers. They used to read to us the story of Joseph and cry over it, and made much of the coat of many colours, and when we came to "your father, the old man of whom ye spake, is he well?" our brawny fathers sobbed and pretended to be only coughing. If anybody had then told us what some people tell us now, that there was no Joseph-no old man-no coat of many colours-no life in Egypt-no forgiving brethren-no family reconciliation-that it is all a dream, a fantasy, an illusion in colour -I know not in what terms he would have been denounced and with what horror he would have been shunned. Some of us still believe in the history of Joseph ; and when all other " short stories " have run out, this story of Joseph will cxact its tribute of tears from the eyes of far-off generations.

Then in this matter of credulity our quaint old pastors were little better than our mothers. If some modern criticism is true, those old pastors were unconscious impostors. They had not a "doubt" to bless themselves with. They read the Bible and actually believed it, and preached it without a stammer. They used to preach about Daniel and the lions' den, and make us feel heroic in the heroism of the brave young man. Now it turns out that there were no lions, there was no den, and worst of all, there was no Daniel. The book of Daniel is taken away bodily. Yet we are told that the Bible has been given back to us by the critics, and that it is a better Book than we had before. Some of us cannot yet receive this saying. At present we are suffering from a grievous sense of loss. Do not suppose, however, that all the higher critics are of one mind, or that they pursue one method, and do not suppose that every minister has given up Joseph and his brethren, or even Daniel and the lions' den. Broad and indiscriminate statements are apt to be untrue and unjust on all sides of great controversies.

Our dear old pastors used to preach about David, and quotingly call him "the sweet singer of Israel "; and now, according to some, it turns out that David was no singer at all, and that he probably never heard of the psalms which he is supposed to have written. Still more widespread is the havoc made by some ruthless sickles. It is bad enough to lose Joseph and his brethren, Daniel and his den, David and his harp, Jonah and his whale, but these are comparative trifles.

There was, according to some, no Miraculous Conception, no Ministry of Miracles, no Resurrection of Christ. All is idealism, poetry, dream and hazy myth. Bethlehem and Nazareth disappear from what we used to call the sacred page. In the old, old time, when we were very young, the Christian Church had a heaven and a hell, an immortal soul, a direct revelation from heaven, a book which it called " The Word of God." In those early days we thought ascended ones were " forever with the Lord." We said in a sob which was really a song, " They shall hunger no more, neither thirst any more, neither shall the sun light on them, nor any heat. The Lamb which is in the midst of the throne shall feed them, and lead them unto living fountains of water, and God shall wipe away all tears from their eyes." We said that each of them had a crown, a harp, and a white robe. Now we are told that all we supposed to be real was but fancy, mirage, and " the stuff that dreams are made of."

I want you to see that if we yielded to these suggestions and demands, we should be giving up a good deal. Do not suppose that it is easy for the soul to part with its very self-with all the things which would leave only emptiness and mocking echoes behind. Some of us have not even yet given up our faith. Blessed be God, some of us still believe in the whole Bible. We know that translation may have its faults, and that copyists may make blunders, and yet we hold to the whole Book-we still call it The Holy Bible; it is to us in substance and in effect the veritable Word of God.

Yes; we have been asked to give up a good deal, and what, as I have already said, aggravates us most of all, is that we have been asked to believe that the giving of it up has made the Bible more precious than ever to us. Genesis turns out to be mainly fable ; Abram is not a man, but "an eponymous hero"; Joseph "is not" in another and deeper sense ; Shadrach, Meshech and Abednego are mere dreams and nightmares ; the books of Kings and Chronicles are removed bodily; Ecclesiastes and Solomon's Song do not appear to have been in the Bible-yet notwithstanding all this we are to think of the Bible being "given back " to us more precious than ever. We cannot do so all at once. Our training blocks the way. Early impressions are often indelible. It is hard to regard supposed enemies as all at once our disguised friends. For example, many of us were brought up to believe that Tom Pine was an awful character-nothing short, indeed, of an infidel, blatant, presumptuous, defiant. Tom Paine was a kind of moral typhus, or a malignant form of small-pox. Every man who had a copy of " The Age of Reason" kept it in a secret drawer and lent it at nighttime and under a whispered vow of secrecy. To possess "The Age of Reason" was equal to having an infectious and loathsome disease. Bishop Watson answered " The Age of Reason," but the Bishop is now nowhere. Tom Paine's " soul goes marching on," but the Bishop is forgotten, as if his book were a mere escape of gas. Tom Paine showed wonderful insight, and in a manner anticipated all the higher critics.

For example, Tom Paine said, "Whoever wrote the Pentateuch, Moses had little or nothing to do with it." But some who say this very thing have orthodox chairs in English universities and sign even more articles than thirty-nine, whilst Tom Paine is branded as an infidel and has no professional income. Tom Paine said there were at least two Isaiahs, in other words, that the Isaiah who wrote the first part of the book never wrote the second, and perhaps never knew that a second part was written. Some higher critics say the very same thing today, whilst Tom Paine is still regarded by orthodoxy as a most noxious beast. Poor Bishop Watson is on many sides treated as an evangelical milksop, whilst Tom Paine is lauded as a man of progress and of advanced and modern thought. Still we are told that Tom and his successors have given us "back" the Bible, and that it is now more precious than ever. It is not for me to revile Tom Paine; but I take it upon myself to say that no Tom Paine, notwithstanding all his insight and foresight, ought to be in any Free Church pulpit, and if Tom Paine is there, we ought to eject and denounce him as a man who is making a living under false pretences.

It is not to be wondered at that some of us still cling to the Bible after the illiterate and traditional manner of our fathers and mothers and pastors. Blame our training. Take full account of our antecedents. We drew in our love of the Bible with our mother's milk. The Bible helped some of us when the father died and there was neither coal in the grate nor bread in the cupboard. It sanctified our poverty, our struggles, our desolation. It turned the grave into a garden plot. It put heart into us when all other things failed. The Bible has made us men. We are not to be told that this consolatory (not critical) Bible is still left to us. How long will it be left? Still higher critics may possibly arise in distant years who will purloin this jewel also. Who can say how much of the Bible will be left in half a century? We have a right to be suspicious. Where much has gone, more may go. On the whole, therefore, I am of opinion that it is better to hold the Bible very much as we have always held it, to keep an open mind in relation to all competent and reverent criticism, to cling to the Bible in all its proved consolations and particular results, and to leave many difficulties and perplexities to be settled when, in heaven, we have more time and more light.

There is one test to which I cannot but submit every creed, every religion, every book. What kind of manhood has it-produced? What sort of men did the old Bible grow? What of their aspirations, their service, their sacrifice? They were grand men. Perhaps narrow-minded, perhaps austere, perhaps conservative, but they were honourable, determined, self-sacrificing men. They were men who put themselves to a great deal of trouble for others. They gave away much money. They counted not their lives dear unto them. They liberated slaves, they smashed iniquitous monopolies, they founded missionary societies, they dared fire and sword, pestilence and cruelty. They had not the latest learning on the Pentateuch, Isaiah and the: Apocryphal books, but they gripped the Bible with a nerve of steel. They had immense and miracle-working faith. I believe in my heart that they were more self-sacrificing than many who laugh at their ignorance and condemn their narrowness. They believed in the literal inspiration of the Bible, in the immortality of the soul, in eternal punishment, in the atoning death of the Lord Jesus, and they cried after, if finally they might attain, the holiness of God. They were not critics-they were great workers ; not grammarians-but generous givers ; not pedants but unsparing in benevolence and sacrifice. I judge every religion by the men it makes, and so judged, the Bible has no need to be ashamed of its stalwarts and its heroes. Shall I offend scholars and critics, grammarians and pedants, if I frankly say that merely as such they have next to nothing to do with the Bible? That the Bible has little or nothing to say to them in their academical capacity? The Bible seeks and finds the heart, talks to the spirit when in the deepest humility, goes out after the soul in its penitence and mortal hunger. When the reader is least a grammarian he may be nearest the spirit of the book. Thus saith the high and lofty One that inhabiteth eternity, to this man will I look, to the man that is of a humble and a contrite heart, and that trembleth at My Word." To "tremble" is better than to parse ; in a deep.: and large sense salvation is not of grammar else then only grammarians could have a high place in heaven.

Chapter 4 A
How to Study the Bible

The Synthetic Method, or Bible Study by Books

THERE are seven methods of Bible Study. Of these the first four are primary or elementary. The remaining three are secondary or subsidiary, and relate to the use of three standard compilations or helps to Bible Study-the Bible Dictionary, the Bible Concordance, and the Bible Commentary. The seven methods of Bible Study are

1. The Synthetic Method, or Bible Study by Books.

2. The Parallel Method, or Bible Study by Marginal References.

3. The Topical Method, or Bible Study by Topics.

4. The Typical Method, or Bible Study by Types.

5. The Cyclopaedic Method, or Bible Study by Bible Dictionary.

6. The Microscopic Method, or Bible Study by Concordance.

7. The Explanatory Method, or Bible Study by Commentary.

Before considering the various methods by which we may hope to attain to the mastery of the Bible, it will be well for us to try and form some conception of the Book as a whole. It is important to realise the unity of the Book, and to grasp its central idea. The Bible consists of sixty-six books, written by about thirty-six different authors, during a period of about sixteen centuries. Yet the most distinctive feature of the Book is not the diversity but the unity of its authorship. It is one Mind that is unfolded to us, one Purpose that is disclosed, one Will that is revealed. The Bible is an organism. Its parts are so related that to reject any one book in it is to destroy the symmetry of the whole, for what remains is no longer a body, but a mutilated trunk..

The Bible is a beautiful,. palace built up out of sixty-six blocks of solid marble-the sixty-six books. In the first chapter of Genesis we enter the vestibule, which is filled with the mighty acts of creation. The vestibule gives access to the law courts-the five books of Moses-passing through which we come to the picture gallery of the historical books. Here we find hung upon the walls scenes of battlefields, representations of heroic deeds, and portraits of eminent men belonging to the early days of the world's history. Beyond the picture gallery we find the philosopher's ,-chamber-the book of Job-passing through which we enter the music-room-the book of Psalms-where we listen to he grandest strains that ever fell on human ears. Then we come to the business office-the book of Proverbs -where, right in the centre of the room, stands facing us the motto, " Righteousness exalteth a nation, but sin is a reproach to any people." From the business office we pass into the chapel - Ecclesiastes, or the preacher in his pulpit, and thence into the conservatory-the Song of Solomon with the Rose of Sharon and the Lily of the Valley, and all manner of fine perfumes and fruit and flowers and singing birds. Finally we reach the observatory-the Prophets, with their telescopes fixed on near and distant stars, and all directed toward " the Bright and Morning Star," that was soon to arise.

Crossing the court we come to the audience chamber of the King-the Gospels-where we find four vivid life-like portraits of the King Himself. Next we enter the work-room of the Holy Spirit-the Acts of the Apostles-and beyond that the correspondence-room-the Epistles—where we see Paul and Peter and James and John and Jude busy at their desks, and if you would know what they are writing about, their epistles are open for all to study. Before leaving we stand for a moment in the outside gallery-the Revelation-where we look upon some striking pictures of the judgments to come, and the glories to be revealed, concluding with an awe-inspiring picture of the throne-room of the King.

I—THE SYNTHETIC METHOD, OR BIBLE STUDY BY BOOKS

One of the chief causes of the widely prevalent spirit of religious indifference is the neglect of Bible Study. The study of the Bible is at once an urgent present need and at the same time an abiding eternal need. The Bible affirms the universal government of God and the eternal duration of man. It demands the present doing of the sovereign will of God. The primary purpose of the Bible is not to satisfy the intellect ; but to correct the will. The Bible brings us at once into the immediate presence of God. Our object in reading the Bible is that we may be brought face to face with God.

It is quite certain that the Church of the present day does not read the Bible as it should. We reverence and pay homage to it, but it does not enter into the warp and woof of the life of our souls, as our daily food enters into and builds up the structure of our bodies. Every Christian ministry should be a ministry of the Word. The real business of the Christian minister is to preach the Word, and the real business of the Christian Church is to adorn the doctrine, to make it beautiful and attractive in the eyes of the world, by translating its holy precepts into the practice of daily life. If the Church is to influence the world it must know the Bible. All that is best in the life of the nation today has been derived from the Bible. But unfortunately the Church of the present day does not, and the world in the present day will not, read the Bible. Hence the decay of attendance in the Christian churches, the loss of young people from the Sunday Schools, and the prevailing secularisation of the Lord's Day. If there is ever to be a revival of spiritual life and power and joy in the Christian Church, there must be a new centre of influence for it to spring from, and that centre can be nothing other than a renewed interest in the study of the Eternal Will as revealed in the Eternal Word. No one ever built his life on the Bible model and had to confess that he had made a mistake and that he might have made a better use of his time. All that is highest and best in us has been derived from the inspiration of the Word of God.

One of the main reasons for the decay of interest in the study of the Bible, apart from the pursuit of pleasure and worldly interests, and the pride of intellect which regards the teaching of the Bible as in some sense outgrown by the advance of modern thought, is the old method of reading the Bible in titbits and snippets instead of devoting the necessary time to grasp the scope and sweep of its majestic argument, and reading the Text in the light of the context, the context in the light of its relation to the book in which it is found, and the book in relation to the Bible as a whole.

The remedy for lack of interest in church prayer-meetings, week-night services, and pulpit ministrations is the introduction of a new method of Bible Study, and Bible Teaching, which will put the people in possession of the rich treasures of the inspired Word, and enable them to master the entire content of the English Bible.

Two illustrations may be given in proof of this statement. Some years ago Mr. D. L. Moody induced Dr. James M. Gray, of Chicago, to introduce the subject of Synthetic Bible Study to the notice of the Christian public of Chicago. The suggestion was acted upon. About four hundred persons out of some one thousand present that evening resolved themselves into a Bible Class for the purpose of Synthetic Bible Study. " This class continued to meet regularly once a week," says Dr. Gray," with unabated interest throughout the whole of that fall and winter, and the next year had multiplied into five classes, held in different parts of the city, on different evenings of the week, but under the same teacher (Mr. W. R. Newell), and with an aggregate membership of over four thousand. The year following, this had increased to five thousand, two or three classes averaging separately an attendance of one thousand two hundred to one thousand five hundred. Since that time similar classes have attained a membership approaching two thousand, and one in Toronto to nearly four thousand."

The second illustration is that of the Friday night meetings of the Bible School under the leadership of Dr. G. Campbell Morgan, at Westminster Chapel, London, with its attendance of one thousand two hundred to one thousand five hundred and sometimes nearly two thousand members each week. For three years Dr. Morgan dealt with the content of the books of the Bible, beginning with Genesis and taking a new book each week. For the next three years he dealt with the message of each book, again beginning with Genesis, devoting a whole evening to each book, and thus making a second systematic synthetic study of the entire Bible. This was followed by a third series of connected Bible Studies, in which the narrative portions of the Bible were dealt with in consecutive order under the title of "The Divine Library as Human History," and again the whole Bible from Genesis to Revelation was passed in review.

The remarkable gifts of these great pioneers and leaders in the field of Synthetic Bible Study may be regarded as accounting in some degree for the enormous crowds by which their lectures were attended, but the fact that the theme of their studies was the Bible, the whole Bible,and nothing but the Bible, and that each of them is pre-eminently a "man of the book," indicates the true source of interest and attractiveness in pulpit and class-room, and the direction in which all true ministers of the Word must look if they would reach the-hearts of the people and gather round them congregations of men and women " whose delight is in the law of the Lord."

The synthetic method of Bible Study by books is perhaps the most interesting and the most fruitful of all the methods of Bible Study. It has this great advantage, that it puts the reader into the position of the writer, and enables him to " think God's thoughts after Him " in the very order in which they were originally revealed and in which they originally arose in the mind of the sacred writers. The method is recommended above all others, because it possesses the inestimable advantage of kindling an interest in the study of the Word. It gives us a comprehensive survey of the whole field of truth. It enables us to sweep the horizon and grasp the drift, the purport and the message of the Book as a whole. Other methods are good, but this is the method on which the Book itself was originally composed, and consequently the one which best enables the reader to enter into possession of the mind of the writer. The study of selected passages and disjointed portions of Scripture is perhaps to some extent responsible for the lukewarmness of those who pursue their studies in this way, the discursive method tending to disapate the interest of the reader, which gradually diminishes and dwindles away instead of gathering strength and leading on to mastery.

The following five rules afford a most succinct and at the same time a most complete explanation of what is meant by the synthetic method of Bible Study by books...

Rule 1.-Read the Bible itself, a whole book at a time, and begin with Genesis. A long book like job could be read through without haste in two hours, and the whole sixty-six books in the entire Bible in less than sixty-six hours.

Rule 2.-Read it continuously, right through at a single sitting, without break, interruption or interval.

Rule 3.—Read it thus repeatedly, over and over again, until you have mastered it.

Rule 4.-Read it independently, without consulting other people's interpretation of it until after you have formed your own conclusion as to its aim, purport, content, and message from direct contact and immediate acquaintance with the Book itself.

Rule 5.-Read it prayerfully, gathering your interpretation of it direct from the Spirit of God, Who is present both in the written Word and also in the heart of the devout reader, and Who interprets its meaning to the reader, and prepares the heart of the reader to receive it.

An excellent illustration of the nature of this method of Bible Study is quoted by Dr. James Stalk in the " Bible Readers' Manual," in which he writes of one who said : " I remember perfectly well the first time I ever read an entire book of Scripture at one sitting. I chanced on a Sabbath to be in a continental country, and in a town in which there was no Protestant service of any kind. In the early morning I had gone to the Roman Catholic service, but it was before breakfast, and I was thrown on my own resources for the rest of the day. Strolling out behind the hotel, I lay down on a green knoll, where I remained the whole forenoon. I opened the New Testament, and dipped into the pages here and there, till chancing on the Epistle to the Romans, I read on and on right through it. As I proceeded I caught the spirit of St Paul's mighty theme, or rather was caught by it, and was drawn on to read. The argument opened out and rose like a great work of art above me, till at last I was enclosed within its perfect proportions. This was a new experience. I saw for the first time that a book of the Bible is a complete discussion of a single subject; I felt the full force of the whole argument; and I understood the different parts in the light of the whole as I had never done when reading them by themselves."

Dr. Gray relates a similar experience on the part of an American layman. "He had gone into the country to spend the Sabbath with his family on one occasion, taking with him a pocket Copy of Ephesians, and in the afternoon, going out into the woods and lying down under a tree, he began to read it ; he read it through at a single sitting, and finding his interest aroused, read it through again in the same way, and, his interest increasing, again and again. I think he added that he read it some twelve or fifteen times, and when I arose to go into the house, said he, I was in possession of Ephesians, or better yet, it was in possession of me, and I had been lifted up to sit in heavenly places in Christ Jesus in an experimental sense in which that had not been true in me before, and will never cease to be true in me again. Thus to master book after book is to fill the mind with the great thoughts of God."

In pursuing this method our first object is to discover the scope of the book, to make a telescopic survey of the subject it deals with, or the ground it covers, to get a bird's-eye view of the whole extent of the book in order to obtain a clear and a comprehensive general idea of its plan, structure, and content, and a vivid impression of its main tenor and general drift. This will enable us to discover the underlying spiritual purpose for which it was written. Every book in the Bible has an object as well as a subject, and usually there will be some keyword or phrase or verse indicating the scope and purpose of the book, and giving the clue to its interpretation.

Each book in the Bible was written for some definite, specific purpose, and was intended to guard the Church in all ages against some definite, specific error. For example, Romans was written in order to guard the Church in all ages against the erroneous doctrine of salvation by works, or merit, or desert, or to make it quite plain to all mankind that God is just as ready to forgive the very worst man that ever lived, as He is to forgive any other member of the race. Similarly, 1 Corinthians is written against rationalism, Galatians against ritualism, and so on, the whole Bible forming a complete armoury whence we may obtain the necessary weapons with which to ward off the attack of any and every spiritual foe.

The results of the application of this method of Bible Study are manifold. In the first place, it is the one method which succeeds best in kindling interest in the Word of God itself. The Bible is without exception the most interesting Book in the world. It is taken from life. It touches life on every side. It puts us into touch with the facts of life. It enables us to see life, to see it steadily, to see it whole, and to see it with the eyes with which God sees it. Not only does this method increase our interest in the Bible, it also deepens our reverence for it and awakens within us the conviction that it is indeed the very Word of God. It is true to fact, true to life, true to God, and true in every part. It produces further a broadening of the mental vision, a quickening of the intellectual powers, a strengthening of the moral powers, and a , deepening of spiritual life. When read in this way the Bible becomes a new Book to us. It is seen to possess an overwhelming interest. It discloses powers of fascination and elements of romance that fill the soul with wonder and delight. It secures the leading of a pure life. It fills the Christian with ardent missionary interest and keen desire to work for Christ. It produces a new sense of the unity and harmony of the whole Bible, a new feeling of its Divine authority.

The synthetic method of Bible Study is also of great value in clearing up the obscurities connected with difficult passages, which yield their true meaning at once when they are seen in their proper place in the entire structure to which they belong. Thus for instance the difficult passages, Hebrews 6: 4-6 and 10: 26-31, are best understood in the light of the drift of the whole epistle, as a warning against the perils of apostasy from Christianity back to Judaism.

The best text-books and examples of the application of the synthetic method of Bible Study are Dr. J. M. Gray's "Synthetic Bible Studies" (Revell, 6s. net) ; Moorhead's " Outline Studies in the Old Testament" (Revell, 3s. 6d. net), and his four volumes of "Outline Studies on the New Testament " (Revell, 3s. 6d.each net) ; Dr. G. Campbell Morgan's "Analysed Bible " (3 vols., Hodder & Stoughton, 3s. 6d. each) containing his lectures on the Content of each book in the Bible, and his "Messages of the Bible " (3 vols., Hodder & Stoughton, 3s. 6d. each) containing his lectures on the Message of each book to the men of our own age. Dr. Gray, Dr. Moorhead and Dr. Morgan have applied the synthetic method to every book in the entire Bible. They have given us the results of their labours in the above-mentioned works.

An auxiliary method of study standing in part outside the synthetic method, and in part embracing it, is the study of Bible Introduction. This method is well expressed in the lines of Solomon Glassius "The author, scope, occasion, theme, time, place and next the form. These seven, let him attend, that reads the text."

The study of Bible Introduction is a useful adjunct to the synthetic study of the Bible, and to some extent involved in it; but it is for the most part a subordinate study and it must never he allowed to occupy valuable time which might be better spent in the synthetic study of the Bible itself. Nor must it ever be regarded as a necessary preliminary thereto. Time spent in the pursuit of auxiliary and subsidiary studies, on questions of date, authorship, and composition, largely speculative and indeterminable, is not well spent, if it means that in pursuing these subordinate studies we thereby deprive ourselves of the time and strength we require for the study of the Bible itself. Where it is found practicable the following divisions are recommended:

1. Writer.

2. Readers.

3. When written.

4. Where written.

5. Character.

6. Content.

7. Canonicity.

" Character," which corresponds with Synthesis, should be sub-divided into (1) Scope; (2) Purpose ; and (3) Keyword. "Content" corresponds with, Analysis, and may be so exhibited as to include Chapter Summary. Synthesis involves Analysis, and is necessarily preceded by it. Analysis or Content is the division of a book into its main, branch, and subdivisions, according to, the nature and structure of the subject-matter with which it deals, with a view to the study of their separate parts, as integral elements, and in their genetic connection. Chapter Summary is the application of the synthetic method to each individual chapter. The content of each chapter may be summarised and arranged under the following seven heads

1. The principal subject of the chapter. '

2. The leading lesson of the chapter.

3. The best verse in the chapter.

4. The prominent persons in the chapter.

5. The references to Christ in the chapter.

6. The reader's resolve, or the practical result obtained by the application of the teaching of the chapter to the discipline of the will and the direction of the reader's own personal life.

7. The personal prayer or the spiritual desire awakened in the heart of the reader and pleaded before God as a result of the reading of the chapter and meditation thereon.

Chapter Summary may be pursued in a formal and mechanical way without much edification or profit, but it may also be carried out in such a way as to yield an accurate detailed knowledge of the facts contained in each chapter of the Bible, a useful discipline for the will, and a fruitful quickening of the devotional life.

ILLUSTRATIONS

I.-A SYNTHETIC STUDY OF THE Books OF THE OLD TESTAMENT

I. The Pentateuch

(1) Genesis is a book of beginnings. It is the seed-plot of the whole Bible. It relates the history of creation, the fall, the flood, and the beginning of the nations. It gives the biography , of Abraham, Isaac, Jacob, and Joseph, and the, beginning of the nation Israel. It covers a period of two thousand two hundred and ninetyeight years from the creation of Adam to the going down into Egypt, where Exodus resumes the story, and seventy-one years beyond, viz to the death of Joseph. Altogether two thousand three hundred and sixty-nine years in addition to the ages before Adam. The purpose of the book is to reveal the will and purpose of God in creation and redemption, from the creation of the world to the beginning of national life in Israel. The keyword of the book is the word "generations," which means issue, descendants, posterity, that is, persons and things created, originated, or produced. (Gen. 2: 4, 5:1, 6: 9; 10:1; 11:10,27; 25:12,19; 36:1,9;37:2)

(2) Exodus relates the story of the deliverance from Egypt, the journey through the Red Sea and the Wilderness, and the giving of the Law at Sinai. It covers a period of two hundred and fifteen years. Its purpose is to trace the history of redemption from the beginning of national life in Israel to the erection of the Tabernacle, one year after the exodus. Its keywords are " redemption by blood,", "a redeemed people," " deliverance by power."

(3) Leviticus is a book of laws. A technical treatise-law codified for the priests. It covers a period of one month. Its purpose is to reveal God's method of dealing with sin. The entire book is fragrant of Christ. Every sacrifice, every garment, every ceremony points to Him. Its permanent message is "The remission of sins can only be given through the shedding of innocent blood."Its keywords are "sin," "sacrifice," " atonement," "priesthood," "holiness," "access," " worship," " communion," "fellowship with God."

(4) Numbers is a book of journeyings and murmurings, pervaded by the spirit of rebellion ; a book of pilgrimage and warfare, of wanderings in the wilderness and grievings of the Spirit of God. Its

central figure is Moses. Its subject matter is partly narrative and partly legislative law codified for the Levites. It covers a period of about thirty-eight years.Its purpose is to reveal the natural depravity of the human heart, especially its proneness to fall into "the sin that doth so easily beset us," viz. the sin of unbelief, and to illustrate the patience of God in His dealings with sinful men. Its central thought is that of service, walk, probation, discipline, and preparation for warfare. Its lesson-beware of unbelief. Its keywords are "journeyed," "murmured," " rebelled." '

(5) Deuteronomy is a book of recapitulation and review. It is Moses' farewell to Israel—law codified for the people. It contains five addresses and nine charges, or fourteen speeches by Moses and two charges by Jehovah-sixteen speeches in all. It is full of urgent exhortations and solemn warnings couched in terms of the utmost tenderness and the greatest severity. It is one long urgent plea for hearty obedience to God, based on the twofold motive of love and fear. It contains some very remarkable prophecies respecting Christ (Deut. 18.), and the future of Israel (Deut. 28), which have been most strikingly fulfilled. It covers a period of one month, the last month but one of the forty years in the Wilderness, the last month of all being the thirty days' mourning for Moses.Its purpose is to reveal God's holy love, the sole and sovereign motive of God's government of man and man's love to God, the only and the all-sufficient motive of man's obedience to God. Its aim is didactic, homiletic, practical. It reviews the past with an eye to the future.Its keywords are "read,"," learn," "teach," " do," " observe," and " obey "-the " law," " commandments," " statutes," and " judgments" of the Lord.

2. The Historical Books

(1) Joshua is a book of the conquest of Canaan, and the division of the land amongst the twelve tribes. It is the " Ephesians " of the Old Testament. It is the story of a military cam paign typifying the warfare of the spirit. It covers a period of about twenty-five years. Its purpose is to reveal the faithfulness of God, and the fulfilment of His promise respecting the possession of the land ; to teach that God is always at war with sin, and executes His righteous judgments upon men and nations, who, by their colossal wickedness, revolting immorality, and atrocious cruelty, have filled their cup of iniquity to the full ; to teach the lesson of unbounded faith and unfailing courage, in conflict with the enemies of God. Its keywords are " victory " and " possession." " Be strong and of a good courage." "

conquer," " possess," " divide," and " inherit " the land, which is yours, not by right of conquest, but by the gift of God.

(2) Judges is a book of relapse and recovery. It relates the story of Israel's progressive national decay from the death of Joshua to that of Samson, under the perpetually recurring fourfold cycle of apostasy, oppression, repentance, and recovery.` We have six apostasies, six servitudes, six cries to God, and six deliverances. Also one attempted deliverance ending in failure. The book covers a period of about three hundred and ninety years. Its purpose is to reveal the perpetual proneness of the human heart to fall away from God, and the everlasting faithfulness of Jehovah, Whose love never fails and Who is always ready to pardon and to deliver those who repent and return to Him; to reveal the fact that God does punish sin, that righteousness exalts whilst sin enslaves. Its keywords are "forsook," "sold," "cried," "delivered," "sin," " punishment," "repentance", "deliverance," "backsliding," "failure," " crime."

(3) Ruth is a charming idyll, forming a third appendix to judges 1:16., and an introduction to 1 Samuel. It is an illustration of piety and purity, in the midst of unfaithfulness and degeneracy, and in striking contrast to the two preceding appendices on idolatry (Judges 17-18) and immorality (Judges 19-21). It covers a period of ten years and a harvest season. Its purpose is to reveal God's plan of redemption, in the rejection of the Jews and the calling of the Gentiles. Boaz the kinsman-redeemer is a type of Christ, and his union with Ruth, the Moabitess, prefigures the betrothal of the Gentiles; to complete the genealogy of the " seed," who is to be of the tribe of Judah (Gen. 49:10) and, as subsequently revealed, of the family of David (2 Sam.7: 12-16); to give a picture of the family life of the pious ancestors of David. Its keyword is " goel," that is, kinsman-redeemer, which is found in it twenty-five times.

(4) 1 Samuel is a book of the establishment of the monarchy. It is occupied with the story of Eli, the ark in captivity, Samuel, Saul, and the life of David before he came to the throne. It covers a period of a hundred years. Its purpose is to reveal the universal sovereignty of Jehovah, and His method of redemption by means of a Messiah, i.e. an anointed. king. Moses founded a theocracy and a priesthood. Samuel founded a monarchy and a line or succession of prophets, official representatives of the hidden yet sovereign theocratic rule of Israel's invisible King. The prophets make and unmake the kings and prescribe the limits within which the supreme temporal power delegated to them is to be exercised. Their chief function was to

foretell the coming of Christ and to prepare the way for Him. Its keywords are " Messiah "-i.e. Christ, i.e. anointed, or appointed, or invested with Divine authority-" king," "kingdom," "reign," "rule."

(5) 2 Samuel tells the story of the reign of David. The king given in anger is taken away in wrath (Hosea 13:11), and the kingdom is transferred from Benjamin to Judah. David is presented as the ancestor and type of Christ, whom he resembles in his sufferings, his prudence, his exaltation, his magnanimity, and his dependence on God. The book contains also a faithful record of David's terrible sin and its awful consequences. It covers a period of forty years. Its purpose is to reveal God's method of redemption by a Messiah Who is to be the " seed " of the woman, the seed of Abraham, the seed of Isaac, the seed of Jacob, the Shiloh or sceptre-bearing descendant of Judah (Gen.3:15, 12:18, 26:4, 28:14 and 49:10), but also the seed of David, the true temple-builder, and the Son of God, in Whom David's house and kingdom and throne shall be established for ever (2 Sam.7: 12-16). These are the sure mercies of David (Is.4:3, Ps. 89: 20-37). To reveal the inconceivable malignity, the iron grip, the irretrievable consequences, and the bitter end of sin, and to enforce the terrible warning-" Be sure your sin will find you out." Its keywords are " Messiah," " Christ," "anointed king" (the word king occurs two hundred and seventy-eight times), "kingdom," " reign," " rule."

(6) 1 Kings is a book of the external history of the kings of Israel and Judah from Solomon to Ahab and Jehoshaphat. Side by side with the secular order of kings, there is a sacred order of prophets. Between the two orders we observe an ever-widening gulf. Also the division of the kingdoms is paralleled by a schism between the prophets. Compare the man of God from Judah and the old prophet of Bethel (1 Kings 13.). Also Micaiah and the four hundred false prophets of Jehovah (1 Kings 22). The history is told from the religious or prophetic point of view. The leading interest centres in the contest between Jehovah and Baal, and the controversy between Jehovah and his people. The book covers a period of about one hundred and twenty years. Its purpose is to reveal the failure of government by kings, the gradual decay of the people, owing to their perpetual proneness to fall away from God, into idolatry and immorality and apostasy, tempered in the case of Judah by occasional reformations and revivals of true religion ; to show that without true religion there can be no pure morality, and that without pure morality there can be no true national greatness or

enduring stability. Its keywords are " between two opinions," "divided," "rent," "disruption," "schism."

(7) 2 Kings is a book of the decline and fall of Israel from Ahaziah to Hosea, and the fall of Samaria, and of Judah from Jehoram to Zedekiah, and the destruction of Jerusalem. To this period belongs the rise of prophecy. Elijah and Elisha, Isaiah, Jeremiah, Ezekiel, Daniel, Hosea, Joel, Amos, Obadiah, Jonah, Micah, Nahum, Habakkuk, and Zephaniah all belong to the period of 2 Kings. The principal topics of the book are the translation of Elijah, the ministry of Elisha, the passing of Israel, and the passing of Judah. It covers a period of about three hundred and twenty years, but the last four verses record an incident which occurred twenty-five years later. Total about three hundred and forty-five years. Total for 1 and 2 Kings about four hundred and sixty-five years. Its purpose is to reveal the failure of kingship, to arrest the progress of national corruption, to prevent the consummation of the process of national degeneration and decay issuing in the overthrow and. the ruin of both.kingdoms, owing to the perpetual proneness of both kings and people to forget God and to forsake His laws, and to show that the God of grace is also a God of judgment. There is no direct prophecy relating to Christ in 1 and 2 Kings, but " to Him give all the prophets witness," and nearly all the prophets are here. Its keywords are rejected," " cast away," " cast out of sight," " carried away into captivity to Babylon."

(8) 1 Chronicles is a genealogical chart and an ecclesiastical or spiritual history of the people of God from Adam to Ezra, written some time after the return to Jerusalem at the end of the seventy years of captivity in Babylon, perhaps by Ezra himself. The genealogy is preserved with a view to the restoration of the returned remnant to their ancient patrimony. The royal line of David is preserved because it contains the ancestors of the Messiah. The rank and station of the priests and Levites are given with a view to their resuming their proper office and ministry. The history of the reign of David is written from the inner spiritual or Divine standpoint. Its chief interest centres in the temple, its officers and services. It covers a period of three thousand one hundred and two years from Adam to Solomon. Its purpose is to reveal the sovereign choice or election of God as illustrated in the selection of Seth, Shem, Abraham, Israel, Judah, and David, not one of whom were the eldest sons of their fathers, as the channel of Divine redemption and blessing to the race ; to magnify God and lead the people to give

Him His right place in the life of the nation. Its keyword is the "
House of the Lord."

(9) 2 Chronicles is an ecclesiastical- or inner spiritual history of the
people of God, from Solomon to Zedekiah, closing with a brief
mention of the proclamation of Cyrus (repeated in Ezra 1: 1-3), It
deals principally with the religious character of the kings, the four
great, national religious revivals, and the varying fortunes of the
House of the Lord. It covers a a period of four hundred and thirty-
six years, or if we include the last three verses, fifty years more, and
the entire book of 1 and 2 Chronicles three thousand five hundred
and eighty-eight years from Adam to Cyrus. Its purpose is to reveal
the failure of government by kings, apart from government by God
to reveal the active participation of the hand of God, in the external
events of history, as seen in His administering defeat to those who
forsook Him, giving the victory to those who relied upon Him for
help ; to show that the rise and fall of men and nations are
determined by the laws which govern the revival and the decay of
religious life; to teach the lesson of the vital necessity of real
religion. Its keyword is the " House of the Lord " ; the " priests," the
"Levites " and the " temple choir " are also prominent.

(10) Ezra tells the story of the return of about fifty thousand exiles
under Zerubbabel and Joshua, the rebuilding of the temple, the
return of about two thousand exiles under Ezra and Ezra's great
religious revival, an attempt to separate the remnant that returned
from all heathen influences, and to restore the ancient theocratic
government of God. It contains numerous references to the priests,
the Levites, and the Nethinims, and several genealogical registers. It
covers a period of twenty-one years (see the author's "Romance of
Bible Chronology "). To this period the prophets Haggai and
Zechariah belong. Its purpose is to record the fulfilment of the
promise of God, that at the end of seventy years the people should
return to their own land (Isaiah 44:28 , 45:1, Jer. 25: 12, 29: 10); to
reveal the universal sovereignty and the everlasting faithfulness of
God, and to give an assurance of the ultimate fulfilment of all His
promises respecting Messiah, people, and land ; to show that God
controls the causes that mould the events of history, in response to
the faith of those who rely upon Him. Its keywords are the " House
of the Lord" (twenty-five times) and the "Temple of the Lord " (six
times). Total, thirty-one times.

(11) Nehemiah is a history of Nehemiah's visit to Jerusalem, the
rebuilding (or rather the repair) of the wall of Jerusalem, in spite of

the opposition of Sanballat, the great religious revival of Ezra and Nehemiah, the sealing of the covenant, the repeopling of Jerusalem, the dedication of the wall and Nehemiah's subsequent visit, and later reforms respecting the sanctity of the House of God, the maintenance of its worship, Sabbath observance, and heathen wives. It covers a period of fifteen years. (See the author's " Romance of Bible Chronology.") The prophet of the closing years of this period, and of the age immediately succeeding it, is Malachi. Its purpose is to reveal the fulfilment of the promise of God (Jer. 29:10-14, 30: 3, 32:. 26-44) in the rebuilding of the wall of Jerusalem, in restoring the remnant to their own city, and protecting them against their foes ; to give an example of true and noble patriotism. Its keywords are the "wall" of Jerusalem, " Arise and build," " I am doing a great work, so that I cannot come down."

(12) Esther is the inspired account of a dramatic incident which occurred at a great crisis in the history of the Jews, when the entire race was in danger of being blotted out of existence. Haman plots against the Jews whom he would exterminate by massacre in one day. Instructed by Mordecai, Esther risks her life and secures for her people the right to act in self-defence on the one lawfully appointed day of the massacre. By risking her life a second time she secures the further right to act in self-defence against any unlawful attack or riotous outbreak on the following day. The book covers a period of ten years. Its purpose is to reveal the fact of the hidden secret working of the sovereign power of God in overruling and co-ordinating the contrary wills of men, so as to make them subserve His own ends, which include the providential preservation of the race from which the Messiah was to spring ; to explain the origin of the Feast of Purim, instituted on this occasion, and observed by the Jews in memory of it, in every country, ever since. The keyword is " the lot is cast into the lap ; but the whole disposing thereof is of the Lord " (Prov 16: 33).

3. The Poetical Books

(1) Job is a handbook, of practical philosophy, a dramatic poem on the problem of pain, a practical, philosophical discussion of the origin of evil, dealing with the real experiences of a historic person. Eliphaz speaks from personal experience as the depositary of a Divine revelation. Bildad appeals to tradition and the wisdom of the ancients. Zophar argues from the deliverances of reason and conscience and the private judgment of the individual. All alike assert that job's sufferings are sent by God as punishment for his

sin. This job denies, and protests his innocence and sincerity. Elihu maintains that suffering is educational, chastening, disciplinary. The problem is left unsolved because it is insoluble. Its purpose is to reveal the fact that evil is by its very nature unaccountable. To explain it is to justify it. No philosophical theory can be framed to account for it without falling into self-contradiction. The solution of the problem is to be found not in the region of thought but in a deed of the Almighty, an actual putting forth of the redeeming activity of God. Man's highest wisdom is to confess his ignorance and sin, and patiently wait for the redemption of God. Its keyword is " patient in tribulation," " Thy will be done","though He slay me, yet will I trust in Him", "shall not the judge of all the earth do right?"

(2) psalms is a collection of spiritual songs forming a handbook of practical devotion. David is the founder of a new order and the originator of a new style of sacred Scripture, viz. poetry set to music for the purpose of devotion. The psalms set forth the attitude of the soul in the presence of God, when contemplating past history, present experience, and prophetic hopes. They celebrate the majesty of God, His goodness and mercy, the kingdom of the Messiah, His sufferings and glory, the wonders of creation, the perfections of the Law, the history of Israel, and the experiences of the individual soul. They are divided into five books, " not according to authorship, or chronology, or the use of the Divine names, but according to the prevailing tone of the devout life which they breathe, rising progressively from darkness to light, from despair to triumph, from prayer to praise. They voice the experience of the godly soul, disturbed and distressed by frequent relapses into sin, but always rising again into a happy and joyous sense of forgiveness and restoration to communion with God. Its purpose is to reveal God as the one true object of love and worship ; to kindle in every soul a sense of the immediate presence of God ; to provide a hymn-book or manual of public worship and private devotion for the Church of God in all ages ; to reveal the presence of indwelling sin in the heart of the godly, and to exhibit the emergence of a deeper sense of sin as a stage of spiritual growth in the realisation of the holy life ; to kindle the aspiration of the soul after holiness, and to confirm the assurance of ultimate victory over sin on the part of those who seek with broken spirit and contrite heart the pardoning mercy and the redeeming grace of God; to lead the soul into a state of perfect trust in the wisdom and goodness of God, in spite of the most bitter experiences of suffering, affliction, and distress ; to reveal the eternal majesty of the unchanging God and the universal glory of the kingdom of the Messiah; to celebrate the power and goodness of

God in creation and in His providential care for His people to reveal the perfect rest and satisfaction and joy of the soul as it draws near and enters into the very presence of God, and obtains the beatific vision of His glory ; to attune the soul to the strain of perpetual praise. Its keywords are " rejoice," " sing," " worship the Lord in the beauty of holiness," "hallelujah, praise ye the Lord."

(3) Proverbs is a handbook of practical morality, a miscellany of master-sentences containing moral truths of practical wisdom for the regulation of conduct. The Hebrew word " Proverbs " means " Governors." Proverbs is the business man's vade-mecum, his guide to honour and happiness and success. It celebrates the value of wisdom and prudence and virtue. What Moses, Samuel, David, and Ezra are to the Law, the prophets, the psalmists, and the scribes, that Solomon is to the wise men (Jer.18:18). He is the founder of a new order, the creator of a new style of sacred literature. - His wisdom is not worldly but heavenly. Its purpose is to reveal the pre-mundane existence and personality of " wisdom as the ultimate foundation of all true morality, the hidden source of all true piety, the eternal possession and daily delight of the Creator (Prov.8:23-36); to inculcate and to impart wisdom ; to furnish "laws from heaven for life on earth"; to show that in the stupendous conflict between good and evil, wisdom and folly, the mastery over the opposing forces can only be obtained by true piety or the " fear of the Lord." Its keywords are "wisdom," " instruction," "understanding," "justice, " "judgment," " equity," "knowledge," " prudence," ".discretion," " the fear of the Lord."

(4) Ecclesiastes is a treatise on the value of life from the standpoint of the man of the world. It probes the depths of the human heart. It traverses the range of human thought. It exhausts the possibilities of human experience. It assays the entire content of human life in the endeavour to find a solution to the problem "How to be happy without God." But the problem is found to be insoluble. The attempt ends in failure and, disappointment, leading to despair. The conclusion is, " Fear God, for in Him alone is found true satisfaction for man's never-dying soul." Its purpose is to reveal the utter emptiness and vanity of all earthly objects and pursuits, and the utter inability of all earthly enjoyments to satisfy the deepest longings of man's immortal soul. The heart is too large for the object. The whole world cannot satisfy it. God has set; eternity (A.V. the world) in the heart (Eccles. 3:11), and nothing but the Eternal God can satisfy man's eternal need.Its keywords are "all," "ever," "every," " the world," " eternity," " God."

34

(5) The Song of Solomon is an idyll, or rather a suite of seven idylls woven into a beautiful unity. It enshrines the constancy of a rustic maiden of Shunem to her betrothed shepherd lover when tempted to transfer her affections to King Solomon. In form it is poetry not prose, oriental not occidental, an idyll not a drama. Its figures are symbols not images, and the true; interpretation of the poem is not the literal and not the allegorical but the symbolic or typical.Its purpose is to reveal the incomparable strength of a chaste and sincere affection, which no splendour can dazzle and no flattery seduce; to reveal the purity, the sanctity, and the eternity of true love ; and to set forth, under the figure of the bride and bridegroom in an earthly love story, the supreme loveliness of Christ-the object too large for the heart-and the inseparable attachment between Jehovah and Israel, Christ and the Church, the soul and its Saviour. Its keywords are "my beloved is mine," " I am my beloved's," " His desire is toward me," " come, my beloved," " make haste, my beloved."

4. The Major Prophets

(1) Isaiah is the evangelical prophet. In Part I- (chapters 1-35) he bewails the awful corruption of Judah, predicts the birth of Immanuel, pronounces the doom of heathen nations and the woes of Israel and Judah. In Part 2 (chapters 36-39) he predicts Judah's deliverance from Assyria, and foretells her captivity in Babylon. In Part 3 (chapters 40-46) he announces her return from Babylon to her native land. The entire book is shot through and through with Messianic references, each subject dealt with ending in a climax, introducing the millennial era of Messiah's rule, Part 3 forming the grand climax of the whole. Its purpose is to reveal the principle and method of God's work in redemption through the virgin birth, vicarious sufferings, propitiatory sacrifice, and atoning death of the Messiah, and His return to execute judgment on the wicked, to establish peace on earth, to rule in righteousness, and to be the Saviour of the world. The book is so full of references to Christ that it has been called " the fifth gospel." Its keywords are " My righteousness," " My salvation."

(2) Jeremiah is the prophet of the broken heart. He prophesied during the reigns of Josiah, Jehoahaz (Shallum), Jehoiakim, Jehoiachin (Jeconiah or Coniah) and Zedekiah, the last five kings of Judah. He fiercely denounces the sins of the people and the folly of their rulers, and pleads with backsliders to return to God. He sends a letter to the captives in Babylon and foretells the fall of Jerusalem.

After its fall, he prophesies to the remnant of the Jews in Judea and Egypt. Then follows a group of prophecies announcing the doom of the nations, and the book concludes with a historical appendix. Its purpose is to reveal the sovereignty of God, the certainty of His judgment and the tenderness of His everlasting love ; to reveal the misery, the tenacity, and the awful corruption of sin, and the coming of a day of salvation when God will write His law in the heart, and the Good Shepherd will lead His people back to God. Its keywords are "lamentation," "weeping," " tears," " the new Covenant."

(3) Lamentations is an acrostic elegy, a dirge, a threnody, or song of overwhelming grief, in five lamentations bewailing the fall of Jerusalem. Each lamentation occupies one chapter. Each chapter contains twenty-two verses, except chapter 3 which has sixty-six verses. In chapters 1-4 inclusive, each verse begins with one of the twenty-two letters of the Hebrew alphabet, in alphabetical order. For the names of these letters see Psalm 119. Chapter 5 also has twenty-two verses, but it is not an alphabetical acrostic like the others. In tone the book of Lamentations is mournful, dirge-like, funereal. In this respect it resembles Gray's " Elegy, or Tennyson's "In Memoriam." Its purpose is to reveal the overwhelming grief and sorrow of the broken heart of our Lord as He hung and died upon the Cross, vindicating at once the incomparable majesty of the moral law and the unfathomable depth of Divine grace ; to reveal at once the holiness of God and His unutterable love for sinful men. Its keywords are " desolation," " weeping," " tears," "behold and see if there be any sorrow like unto My sorrow," " My God, My God, why hast Thou forsaken Me?"

(4) Ezekiel is the prophet of the people of God in exile, the prophet of dazzling visions, of departing and returning glory, of the new birth, the new people, the new land, the new temple, and the new city. He embraces all Israel in his prophecy, and predicts their resurrection, their reunion, and their future glory. His prophecies are methodically arranged in chronological order, except chapter 29., which is grouped with other prophecies relating like itself to Egypt. The method of Ezekiel's prophecies, is that of symbol and. vision. The book abounds in metaphors and parables and allegories and symbolic acts. In this respect it resembles Daniel and Revelation.Its purpose is to reveal the majesty, the supremacy, and the universal sovereignty of God, Who works, through chastisement and judgment, to the restoration of all Israel and the final establishment and consummation of the kingdom of God ; to

sustain the faith of the exiles on the overthrow of the national economy by promises of national restoration. Its keywords are " I will, " I will not," " and ye shall know that I am the Lord " (fifty times), "Son of Man" (ninety-one times).

(5) Daniel is the prophet of Gentile dominion, The first six chapters contain six historic incidents of the reigns of Nebuchadnezzar, Belshazzar and Darius the Mede. The last six chapters contain four apocalyptic visions seen by Daniel in the reigns of Belshazzar, Darius the Mede, and Cyrus. The book covers a period of seventy-two years, viz. the seventy years of the Babylonian captivity and the two following years. Its purpose is to reveal the method and the times of God's government of His people, under the dominion of the Gentile rulers of Babylon, Medo-Persia, Greece, and Rome ; to indicate the time of the advent and crucifixion of the Messiah, and to give, in outline, a symbolic representation of the history of the world from the Babylonian exile to the establishment of the kingdom of God on earth ; to sustain the faith of the people of God, during times of tribulation, by inspiring examples of noble daring, unflinching courage, immovable faith, and unwavering loyalty to God. Its keyword is " the everlasting dominion of the Son of Man."

5. The Minor Prophets

(1) Hosea is the prophet of mercy. He proclaims the loving-kindness and . tender mercy of Jehovah toward backsliding Israel. He prophesied during the seventy years that preceded the fall of Samaria and the end of the Northern Kingdom, after which, there was a period of seventy years of prophetic silence between the close of the ministry of Isaiah and the prophetic call of Jeremiah. The first three chapters of Hosea are parabolic. Hosea's love for his adulterous wife Gomer, who deserted him for a life of shame, and was sold into slavery, and afterwards redeemed by Hosea and shut up for many days, is an acted parable of Jehovah's inextinguishable love for idolatrous Israel. The names of Hosea's wife and children are likewise symbolic and prophetic of God's method of dealing with His people. Its purpose is to reveal Jehovah's lovingkindness and tender mercy to backsliding and idolatrous Israel, His everlasting faithfulness, and His unquenchable love for the sinful, the erring, and the lost. Its keywords are " Gomer" =rotten-ripe, " Jezebel "=scattered, sour, " Lo-ammi" "=repudiated, " Lo-ruhamah "=unpitied, " I will heal their backsliding," " I will love them freely."

(2) Joel is the prophet of religious revival. He writes on the occasion

of a devastating plague of locusts, followed by a desolating drought. This he interprets as a judgment of God. He sounds a clarion call to repentance, in response to which he promises abundant material and spiritual blessing. He announces the outpouring of the Spirit on all flesh, the execution of the judgment of God upon Israel's foes, and the establishment of Jehovah's Kingdom in Zion.. Joel is dramatic, eschatological, telesmatic, apocalyptic. It contains the kernel and strikes the keynote of all subsequent apocalyptic prophecies. Its purpose is to reveal the certainty and the solemnity of the coming "day of the Lord," in grace toward the penitent, in judgment upon the rebellious, and in government over all ; to kindle anew the spirit of real religion in the hearts of the people, by proclaiming the judgment and the grace of Jehovah. Its keywords are " the day of the Lord," "sound an alarm," " I will pour out my Spirit upon all flesh," "the valley of decision."

(3) Amos is the prophet of justice. His book is a well-ordered whole. It begins with a sonnet of eight stanzas on the doom of the nations (chapters 1-2). Then follow three discourses on the corruption of Israel, each beginning, " Hear ye this word" (chapters 3-6). The doom of Israel is disclosed in a series of five visions (chapters 7:1 to 9:10) and the last five verses contain the usual Messianic conclusion. The message of Amos is predominantly a message of doom. He denounces Israel's incurable depravity, not merely a perpetual violation of the laws of humanity, but chiefly as thwarting God's gracious will and purpose in the government of mankind. Its purpose is to reveal the righteous judgment of God upon the sins of Israel-idolatry, immorality, injustice, violence, robbery, and oppression of the poor; to proclaim the down- fall of the throne, the exile of the people, and the dissolution of the State ; to show that moral causes and spiritual forces determine the standing and the falling of men and nations ; and to intimate the raising again of the fallen tabernacle of David. Its keywords are " justice," " righteousness," "hate the evil," " love the good," " let judgment run down as waters, and righteousness as a mighty stream."

(4) Obadiah is the prophet of the doom of Edom. His message, like that of Jonah and Nahum, is exclusively that of the doom of a foreign nation, ending with the usual Messianic conclusion. Obadiah is the shortest book in the Old Testament, and the only book in the Old Testament consisting of one chapter only. It is the original prophecy of the doom of Edam, quoted and enlarged by Jeremiah (49:7-22) and Ezekiel (25:12-14). Compare Psalms 137: 5. The primary reference of Obadiah is to the event alluded to in Amos

1:11 and Joel 3:19. There is also a genuine prophetic reference to the future conduct of Edom at the destruction of Jerusalem by Nebuchadnezzar, the destruction of Jerusalem here foretold being accomplished five years later by Nebuchadnezzar himself. Compare Jer. 52: 29, 30. The words " thou shouldest not" and neither shouldest thou " in Obadiah verses 12 , 13 and 14 must be translated " do not," as in the margin of the A.V., and similarly in the text of the R.V. Its purpose is to reveal the purpose of God for the deliverance and salvation of the house of Jacob, the judgment of Israel's foes, and the establishment of the kingdom of Jehovah upon Mount Zion; to warn the nations in all ages of the perils of Jew-baiting, anti-Semitism, or hatred of the Jew, whose cause God Himself will undertake, and whose enemies He will destroy. Its keywords are " Esau and Jacob," " unbrotherly hate," "vindictiveness," "retribution," " as thou hast done, it shall be done unto thee."

(5) Jonah is the prophet of the doom o f Nineveh averted, the man of anti-missionary spirit who became- the first great missionary to men of other lands, the man of limited outlook, narrow spirit, exclusive sympathies, and perverted patriotism, to whom God reveals the wideness of His mercy, the abundance of His grace, and the universal range of His loving-kindness and tender care, which He extends not only to all men but even to cattle (Jonah 4:11). Jonah is a man, not a myth, a fact not a fable, a type and therefore a reality, not a product of the imagination.. The book is a history not an allegory, a record of fact not a work of fiction. It is the autobiography of a real person, who was a prophet of considerable eminence. Its purpose is to reveal the world-wide range of the purpose of God in redemption, embracing as it did the entire human race; to show that God's covenant with Abraham was that through him all the nations of the earth should be blessed; to reveal the long-suffering forbearance of God, and to rebuke the narrow exclusiveness of His people. Its keywords are "gracious," "merciful," " slow to anger," " of great kindness," " repent," "pity," " spare," " three days and three nights," "life from the pit" (marg.).

(6) Micah is the prophet of justice and mercy He unites in himself the qualities and characteristics of both Amos and Hosea, the stern demands of morality and the free grace of the Gospel, God's truth to Jacob and His mercy to Abraham (chapter 7: 20). His prophecy consists of three addresses, each commencing with " Hear," and each following the same cycle of (i) sin, (2) judgment, and (3) salvation. Its purpose is to reveal Jehovah's purpose of salvation

through the going forth out of Bethlehem of Him Whose goings forth have been from of old from everlasting, and the simplicity of Jehovah's requirements-justice, mercy, and a humble walk with God. Its keywords are " justice," " mercy," " humility " or "piety," " swords into plowshares," " Jehovah's controversy," Micah="who is a God like unto Thee " (chapter 7: 18).

(7) Nahum is the prophet of the doom of Nineveh executed. He should be read along with Jonah, the prophet of the doom of Nineveh averted. The book of Nahum forms one entire whole. It is one continuous embodiment of a single inspiration. It is a vivid, glowing, pictorial, dramatic description of the conflict between Jehovah and the world-empire of Nineveh, with reference to the people of Judah. Its purpose is to reveal the irresistible might and majesty of Jehovah and His unalterable purpose of grace to His chosen people, and of everlasting destruction to the pagan powers that set themselves in battle array against Him; to indicate the ultimate issue of the stupendous conflict between good and evil in the final triumph of Messiah, and the publication of the good tidings of the gospel of peace.Its keywords are " Nahum "= comforter (God comforts His people by executing vengeance on their foes), "vengeance," " an utter end," " good tidings."

(8) Habakkuk is the prophet of the doom of if Chaldea. He belongs to the period of the transfer of the sovereignty of the world from Nineveh on the Tigris to Babylon on the Euphrates. His book is a vivid, dramatic, Joblike challenge to Jehovah to explain the prevalence of evil in a world placed under the universal sovereignty of God. What Habakkuk does," says Luther, "is to caress his people, to take them in his arms, to comfort and cheer them, as one caresses a poor weeping child, or a fellow-creature, that it may be hushed and contented, because it will soon, if God will, be better." Its purpose is to reveal the eternal laws of retribution and progress, the place of faith, and the redeeming activity of God in response thereto, in the great drama of the world's history. To show that however dark the immediate prospect, the ultimate issue will be the establishment of the kingdom of God on earth. Its keywords are "how long?" "why?" " watch," " wait," " believe," " the just shall live by his faith," " God is come," " salvation."

(9) Zephaniah is the prophet of the doom of Judah. His theme is the consummation of the history of the world in the "day of the Lord," a day of judgment and a day of wrath. His description of the Dies Irae (Zeph. 1: 14-18) is unsurpassed in its fierce terrors, as his

description of the blessings of the Divine presence in the restored Jerusalem (Zeph.3:16, 17) is unequalled in its gentleness and beauty. Zephaniah is a compendium of all prophecy. He singles out and enforces the main central truths of all prophecy, omitting local details and temporal agencies, and filling his canvas with an aweinspiring picture of the presence of the Divine Judge Himself. Its purpose is to reveal the method and purpose of the government of God in the judgment of the world, and the issue of the redeeming activity of God in the establishment of His Kingdom-its centre Zion, its kernel Israel, its circumference the world. Its keywords are ".the day of the Lord," ".the day of wrath," "the fierce anger of the Lord," " the Lord thy God in the midst of thee," I will gather," "sing," "shout," be glad," "rejoice."

(10) Haggai is the prophet of the building of the second temple. His prophecy is an inspiration and an encouragement to Zerubbabel the governor, Joshua the high priest, and the remnant of the fifty thousand exiles in Babylon, who had returned to Jerusalem about sixteen years before, to resume and to persevere with the work of the building of the temple. Earlier attempts to build the temple had been frustrated by their adversaries, but at length, owing to the prophecies of Haggai and Zechariah, the foundation of the second temple was laid on the twenty-fourth day of the ninth month of the second year of Darius Hystaspes (521-485 B .C.). Like Ezekiel, Haggai's interest centres in the temple and its ritual, but only as these are earthly symbols of the true worship and spiritual service of the Lord Whose glorious presence ever dwells therein. Its purpose is to reveal the surpassing glory of the latter house as the shrine of Messiah's presence, and the immovable stability of His Kingdom, amid the ruin and the fall of the kingdoms of the world ; to encourage the people to build the temple. Its keywords are "the Lord's house," "the Lord's temple," "consider your ways," "the Desire [= (1) Messiah or (2) silver and gold] of all Nations."

(11) Zechariah, like Haggai, is a prophet of the return from exile. The prophecy of chapters 1-8 is an inspiration and an encouragement to Zerubbabel and Joshua and the returned ,remnant to persevere with the building of the temple, the last two of these chapters containing a reply to an inquiry respecting fasting. Chapters 9-14 is a prophecy of the rejection of the Messiah at His first coming, followed by His second advent and His millennial reign. Its purpose is to reveal the fact that on the completion of the seventieth year from the destruction of the first temple, the time had come for the temple to be rebuilt, and in an undated but later

prophecy, when the incorrigible unfaithfulness of the returned-remnant had become evident, to announce the coming of the Messiah, Who, after being rejected at His first coming, would return again to reign as " King over all the earth." Its keywords are "the temple," " Zion," " Jerusalem," "the angel of the Lord," "the Lord of Hosts," " my servant the Branch," my Shepherd," " Behold thy King."

(12) Malachi is the prophet of the unconscious corruption of the returned remnant and of the faith and piety of the godly remnant of that remnant. The book is a connected, prophetic discourse on the relation of Jehovah to His people. It is addressed to a degenerate people in a decadent age. In form it is a conversation, a dialogue, an expostulation, containing (1) a charge, (2) a reply, (3) a specification, and (4) a sentence, together with a picture of the ideal worship (1:11), the ideal priest (2: 5-7) and the ideal people (3:16-18). Malachi is the "seal" of the prophets. He closes the Canon of the Old Testament with a prediction of the ingathering of the Gentiles (1:11), the mission of the forerunner (3:1 , 4:5), and the advent of the Messiah (3:1, 4: 2,5). Its purpose is to reveal the failure of the old covenant, and to herald the dawn of a new dispensation, i.e. a new method of Divine administration in human affairs, in which the Sun of Righteousness would arise with healing in His wings. Its keywords are " wherein " " weariness," "corruption," " curse," " my name," " my covenant," " my messenger" (Elijah), "the messenger of the covenant " (Messiah).

II.A SYNTHETIC STUDY OF THE BOOKS OF THE NEW TESTAMENT

I. The Four Gospels

(1) Matthew introduces us to Jesus as He is revealed in His words. His genius is typically Jewish. He is characterised by zeal. He writes to unfold the significance of the past. His thought is Biblical, prophetic, culminatory. His style is logical. According to Augustine, his ecclesiastical symbol is the lion. He presents Jesus in His royal aspect as the true Messiah, the King of the Jews. His aim is to convince the intellect. He is influenced by his residence in Judea and his contact with the Apostle James. He writes for Jews living in Judea. He presents Christ as He is revealed to us in His speech, sayings, words, discourses, and doctrines. He appeals in support of the cogency of his argument to the fulfilment in Christ of. the prophecies of the Old Testament. He agrees with James in the

emphasis which he lays on the teaching of Jesus and in his constant appeal to the Old Testament. He has points of contact with Acts 1-7, the early history of the Church in Jerusalem. His keyword is "that it might be fulfilled."

(2) Mark introduces us to Jesus as He is revealed to us in His works. His genius is typically Roman. He is characterised by energy. His thought is vigorous, pregnant, practical. His style is vivid, graphic, impetuous. According to Augustine, his ecclesiastical symbol is the face of a man, but Jerome reverses the symbols and gives to Mark the lion and to Matthew the man (See Ezek. 1:10). Mark's aim is to arouse the will. He is influenced by his travels with Peter. He presents Christ as He is revealed to us in His mighty deeds. He writes for Roman readers and appeals to the Roman sentiment of imperial sovereignty. He reflects Peter's energetic, impulsive, unconventional character. He omits all facts reflecting honour on Peter, but faithfully records instances of his presumption and rebuke. He has points of contact with Acts 8-10, Peter and the Roman centurion Cornelius. His. keyword is " straightway."

(3) Luke introduces us to Jesus as He is revealed to us in His grace. His genius is typically Greek. It is characterised by breadth of sympathy. He writes to reveal the hopefulness of the future. His thought is philosophical and historical. His style is literary and artistic. His ecclesiastical symbol is the ox. He presents Jesus in His sacrificial aspect as the atoning Victim and Saviour of the race. His aim is to touch the heart. He is influenced by his constant companionship with Paul, his literary opportunities, and his later date. He writes for Greeks living all over the world. He presents Christ as He is revealed to us in the grace, tenderness and charm of His silent influence. He appeals in the beauty of his portrait, to the world-wide sympathy of the universal human heart. He reproduces Paul's universal gospel of God's free forgiveness and justification of all by grace through faith. He has points of contact with Acts 13-28, Paul's great missionary journeys. His keyword is " to preach the gospel to the poor."

(4) John introduces us to Jesus as He is revealed to us in His unique personality. His genius is typically oriental. It is characterised by penetration. He writes to unfold the meaning of eternity. His thought is contemplative, intuitional. His style is oracular, peremptory. His ecclesiastical symbol is the eagle. . He presents Christ as He is revealed to us in His Divine glory as the Son of God. His aim is to convince the whole man. He is influenced by his

acquaintance with the facts of our Lord's Judean ministry during the first year of his ministerial life, by his residence in Asia, and by his far later date. He writes as an independent witness, incidentally though not designedly supplementing the synoptics with which he is .acquainted. He writes for Alexandrians and Asiatics in Egypt and Asia Minor. He presents Christ as an embodiment of Divine Life and Light and Love. His appeal is addressed to the faculty of intuition or spiritual vision. His keywords are " witness " and " believe."

2. The Acts

Acts is a book of the continuation of the work which Jesus began but did not complete. It is a book of the activity of the Holy Spirit. It is a book of the growth, expansion, multiplication, and world-wide spread of Christianity (1) numerically (one hundred and twenty three thousand, five thousand, multitudes) ; (2) socially (layman, priests, proselytes and pagans) ; and (3) geographically, from Jerusalem to Judea and Samaria, Antioch, Asia Minor, Europe, and Rome, the centre of the civilised world.

3. The Epistles of Paul

(1)Romans is a treatise on the subject of justification by faith, designed to preserve the Church in all ages against the erroneous doctrine of salvation by works, by merit, or by desert.

(2) I Corinthians is directed against rationalism and pride of intellect, and its consequent sectarian divisions.

(3) 2 Corinthians vindicates the authority of the Apostle Paul to whom was entrusted the revelation of God's purpose in the formation of the Church. It was a vital necessity that the Divine authority of this revelation should be put beyond question.

(4) Galatians defends the gospel of the free grace of God against the advocates of ritualism, ceremonialism, and legalism.

(5) Ephesians reveals to us the exalted position of the believer " in Christ," and the purpose subserved by the Church in the eternal counsel of God.

(6) Philippians sets before us the inward state and the outward

conduct which should characterise normal Christian experience, the keynote of which is struck in the word " rejoice."

(7) Colossians is a defence of the gospel against the ever-present twofold danger of being evaporated into a philosophy or frozen into a form.

(8) 1 Thessalonians is keyed to the expectation of that ever-impending, ever-imminent event-the second coming of our Lord.

(9) 2 Thessalonians embodies a further revelation respecting a subsequent " day of the Lord," and the apostasy by which it is to be preceded.

(10) 1 Timothy sets before us the mind of Christ with regard to sound doctrine and Church discipline during the declension and the disorder of the " latter times."

(II) 2 Timothy gives similar directions with regard to the corruption and the apostasy of the still later " last days."

(12) Titus emphasises the necessity of sound doctrine, but lays more stress on Church order and on the character of the Christian teacher.

(13) Philemon is an illustration of Christian courtesy, combining the utmost tact with apostolic authority.

(14) Hebrews is a treatise on the finality of faith in Jesus Christ, God's Son, the perfect, complete, and final revelation of God to man. The argument for the superiority of Christianity to Judaism turns on the superiority of Jesus Christ, the vehicle of the new revelation, to (1) angels, (2) prophets, (3) leaders, (4) priests, and (5) patriarchs, the vehicles of the earlier revelation. It is interwoven throughout with exhortations and warnings, and the epistle concludes with a majestic appeal to the incomparable power of a living faith in the living God.

4. The General Epistles

(1) James is the most Hebraic and the least distinctively Christian book in the New Testament. It denounces Jewish sins and calls the churches " synagogues." It resembles the Old Testament, especially

the book of Proverbs, and reproduces the teaching of our Lord, especially Matthew's sermon on the Mount. It complements without contradicting Paul's doctrine of justification by faith. James contrasts a living faith which produces works, with a dead faith, i.e. mere intellectual assent which produces nothing. Paul contrasts a living faith which justifies, with works of law , i.e. mere ceremonial observances which justify no man.

(2) 1 Peter links the sufferings of Christ," which are mentioned in every chapter, with the "glory that should follow. It was written to sustain the faith of Christian believers who were undergoing the fiery ordeal of persecution.

(3) 2 Peter deals with the apostasy of those who deny the redeeming value of the atoning death of our Lord, and who scoff at the doctrine of our Lord's return.

(4) 1 John is neither a private letter nor a treatise, but a pastoral address or an encyclical letter to the Churches of Asia Minor. It is characterised by intuitive insight, majestic calm, and contemplative repose. These are combined with absorbing love, burning zeal, and an intensely practical aim. Its main purpose is constructive. It is designed to lead Christians to a conscious realisation of the new life to which they are called in fellowship with Christ, a life at once transcending and vanquishing the world.

(5) 2 John is a letter of a personal and private nature. It lays great stress on the maintenance of the truth, by which is meant the truth revealed in Holy Scripture.

(6)3 John is also a letter of a personal and private character. It deals with a situation of still deeper apostasy in which the authority of the Apostles themselves is challenged and defied. It gives us an insight into the ordinary everyday life of the early Churches, not as we idealise them, but as they really were, with all their excellences and defects, their noble and ignoble features, their meek and their ambitious members.

(7) Jude contemplates " the last time " in which the truths denied are so vital that without them there is no gospel at all. It denounces the false and corrupt teachers who have crept into the Church, and gives solemn warnings against the dangers of backsliding and apostasy.

5. Revelation

Revelation is a book of prophecy. The theme of the whole book is the second coming of our Lord, and the stupendous conflict between the forces of good and evil. It traces the downward course of corruption and apostasy to its final issue in the overthrow of the Evil One, and the consummation of the purpose of God in the final triumph of Christianity over all its foes.

Chapter 4 B

The Parallel Method, Or Bible Study by Marginal References

The division of the Bible into chapters was made by Cardinal Hugo de Sancto Caro, A.D. 1248, but it is quite possible that he copied them from the works of Lanfranc, or from those of Stephen Langton, Archbishop of Canterbury.

The division of the Bible into verses was made by Robert Stephen in 1551, though quite possibly he may have copied the Old Testament verse-divisions from Rabbi Nathan, and the New Testament verse-divisions from some other source.

This division of the Bible into chapters and verses has been frequently criticised. Modern editions, like the Paragraph Bible, the Century Bible (R.V.), and many others are printed in such a way as to obliterate the sharp distinction between verse and verse. They replace the short sentences by the longer paragraph. The chapter and verse divisions of our A.V. are by no means authoritative. In some instances they may be said to be inaccurate and misleading. But there is much to be said for them. They break up the long paragraphs, which suit the taste of the literary student, into short sentences which are more easily grasped, and which appeal more strongly to the understanding of the common people. The translators of our A.V. made it their special aim to render the original in such a manner that each verse should be a perfect gem in itself, capable of being grasped and retained in the memory of the simplest and most unlearned of its readers. In accomplishing this purpose the A.V. has become the household treasure of the common people.

On the whole, the work of dividing the Bible into chapters and verses has been so exceedingly well done that it will never be supplanted by any other. Its convenience for purposes of reference is so great that it may truly be described as indispensable.

It would be interesting to study the growth of the additional matter inserted in the margin of our A.V. The earlier translations of the Bible printed before A.D. 1611 were largely annotated with bitter polemical anti-popery notes, but these were expressly excluded by the instructions of King James I. to the translators of the AV.

The dates placed in the margin of our modern Bibles were first published in Lloyd's Bible (1701). Bishop Lloyd obtained them, in substance, from Archbishop Ussher's "Annals of the Old and New Testaments" (1650-4). They are sufficiently exact to 'be a real help to the reader, but they require to be revised, especially for the period between the Exodus and Samuel, and for that of Ezra and Nehemiah, as the present writer has shown in his " Romance of Bible Chronology " (Marshall Bros., 2 vols).

The notes prefixed by a dagger (t) give the, exact literal translation of the Hebrew and Greek originals. Those prefixed by parallel bars (||) give alternative translations to those contained in the Text. But the bulk of the matter contained in the margin of the A.V. consists of references to other passages of Scripture.

The number of these references to parallel passages, in the original standard edition of the A.V. published in 16 11, was

In the Old Testament- 6,588

In the Apocrypha- 885

In the New Testament-1,517

Total - 8,990

More than half of these are derived from the Latin Vulgate, and preserve for us the fruits of the researches of mediaeval scholars and the traditional expositions of the Western Church. These textual marginal references have been gradually accumulating until to-day the number printed in our modern editions of the A.V. has reached a total of sixty thousand, or seven times the number printed in the original edition of 1611.

John Canne (1682) added a number of references, more suggestive than striking, for the purpose of comment and explanation, on the principle of making the Bible its own interpreter.

Blaney's Bible (1769) added thirty thousand four hundred and ninety-five passages, and further additions were made by Clark (1810) and Scott (1822). Bagster's Bible (1846) contains five hundred thousand references, but this number was so large that it proved to be an encumbrance. Bagster's " Treasury of Scripture

Knowledge" exemplifies the truth that the best commentary on the Bible is the Bible itself, for it contains the substance of all that is best in many commentaries. It is a book of textual references and marginal notes to every verse in the Bible. Dr. Torrey says, " I have found more help in it than in all other books put together." The Religious Tract Society's Annotated . Paragraph Bible (1861) contains a very profitable. collection of texts. The additions made in Dr. Scrivener's Cambridge Paragraph Bible (1873) are rather copious, but admirably designed for practical use.

The marginal references in the R.V. (1898) were compiled by Dr. Scrivener, Dr. Moulton, and the Rev. A. W. Greenup. This is an excellent collection of references embodying the chief results of modern Biblical scholarship in this department.

One of the very best sets of marginal references is the original collection of the Scofield Reference Bible (1909). These references are based not on accidental and superficial resemblances, but on a new system of connected topical references in which all the great truths of Divine revelation are traced through the entire Bible from the place of first mention to the place of last mention, all the references on each topic being linked together so as to form one complete chain. This method imparts interest to Bible Study, and is a more excellent way of arriving at a synthesis of Bible truth than the fragmentary and disconnected study of isolated texts.

The method of Bible Study by parallel marginal references is not to be pursued in a mechanical way. Intelligence and discrimination were exercised by the compilers of the references, and intelligence and discrimination must be employed in the use of them. A careful analysis of the references given in the margin of any ordinary present-day edition of the A.V. will show that they are of several different kinds. Of these seven distinct classes may be enumerated.

1. Quotations or direct citations o f one passage of Scripture in another passage:

Psalm 110:1 : "The Lord said unto my Lord, Sit thou at my right hand, until I make thine enemies thy footstool."

Matthew 22: 43-44: " He saith unto them, How then doth David in spirit call him Lord, saying, The Lord said unto my Lord, Sit thou on my right hand, till I make thine enemies thy footstool? "

Here we have a direct quotation by our Lord in the New Testament of the words of David in the Old Testament, and no ingenuity can ever explain away the fact that the words of our Lord clench the testimony of the psalm title, and confirm the Davidic authorship of Psalm 110.

2. Parallels, in which there is a certain similarity of thought or expression in two independent passages, whether this resemblance be merely verbal or one pertaining to the general sense and meaning o f the passage:

Exodus 13: 21: " And the Lord went before them by day in a pillar of a cloud, to lead them the way ; and by night in a pillar of fire, to give them light ; to go by day and night."

Here the margin of the A.V. gives fourteen additional parallel passages, in which reference is made to the pillar of cloud and fire, viz:

Exod. 14:19: At the crossing of the Red sea.

Exod: 14: 24: After the crossing of the Red sea.

Exod. 40: 38: In the Wilderness.

Num. 9:15: Covering the Tabernacle. Num. 10: 34: Upon the people.

Num. 14:14: Going before the people. Deut. 1: 33: Showing the way. Neh. 9: 12: Leading and giving light. Neh.9:19 : Never departing from them. Ps.78: 14: Leading by day and night. Ps.99: 7: A place from which the Lord spoke.

Ps.105: 39: Covering and giving light.

Isaiah 4:5 : On every dwelling place..

1 Cor 10:1 : Over all " our fathers."

A profitable Bible Study, greatly enriching our knowledge of the Word, will be obtained by searching out all the references to the subject which have been placed together in the margin of the verse in which it is first mentioned.

51

3. Illustrations, in which one passage throws a certain measure of light upon the meaning o f another:

Proverbs 24: 16: "The wicked shall fall into mischief."

Esther 7:10: "So they hanged Haman on the gallows which he had prepared for Mordecai."

Here the general principal or truth of the proverb is illustrated by means of a historical example taken from the narrative portion of Scripture. Instances of this kind are frequently found in the book of Proverbs, which is peculiarly adapted to the purposes of this method of Bible Study.

4. Explanations, in which the meaning o f the original is further elucidated and defined:

Isaiah 6:9-10: "Hear ye indeed, but understand not ; and see ye indeed, but perceive not. Make the heart of this people fat, and make their ears heavy, and shut their eyes lest they see with their eyes, and hear with their ears, and understand with their heart, and convert, and be healed."

This most difficult passage is quoted six times over in the New Testament, viz Matthew 13: 14. Mark 4:12. Luke 8:10. John 12:40. . Acts 28:26. Romans 11: 8.

Each additional reference throws some light upon the original, and tends in some degree to elucidate its meaning, but the passage is still involved in mystery, for it deals, not indeed with 'the unreasonable but with the unrevealed will of God respecting incorrigible unbelief. It is one of those passages which involve the problem of the origin, and the continued existence of evil, and the hidden wisdom and the hidden will of God in relation to it.

5. Interpretations, or fulfilments, in which the meaning of the original is further developed, additional or further truth being incorporated with the truth expressed in the original:

Hosea 11:1 : "Out of Egypt have I called my son." ,

Matthew 2:15: " That it might be fulfilled which was spoken of the Lord by the prophet, saying, Out of Egypt have I called my Son."

Here the words in Hosea are applied to the children of Israel as the people of God, His first-born, whom He called out of Egypt at the time of the Exodus. But the words are true in a deeper sense, and as used by Matthew they become the vehicle of a deeper truth. God calls Israel " my son," " my first-born." But Israel failed to answer the description. Christ is the true representative of Israel. He therefore takes the place of the nation. He is the true " Son " of God, and in Him the prophecy is fulfilled.

6. Adaptations, in which the original thought is modified and exhibited in relation to some new set o f circumstances:

Jeremiah 31:15: : " A voice was heard in Ramah, lamentation, and bitter weeping Rachel weeping for her children refused to be comforted for her children, because they were not."

Matthew 2: 17, 18: "Then was fulfilled that which was spoken by Jeremiah the prophet, saying, In Ramah was there a voice heard, lamentation, and weeping, and great mourning, Rachel weeping for her children, and would not be comforted, because they are not."

Here the promise of the restoration of Israel is announced by the prophet Jeremiah, at a time of bitter weeping and inconsolable sorrow, for the children of Rachel in Ramah. The words are adapted and used to describe the bitter weeping and the inconsolable sorrow of the bereaved mothers of Bethlehem, whose innocent children had been massacred by the cruel sword of Herod.

7. Applications, in which a general truth is brought to bear upon the circumstances of some particular occasion:

Matthew 2: 23: " And he came and dwelt in a city called Nazareth : that it might be fulfilled which was spoken by the prophets, He shall be called a Nazarene.

Here the references given in the margin of the A.V. to Judges 13: 5 and 1 Samuel 1:11 are false and misleading. There is no reference in the text to the vow of the Nazarite (Judges 13:5, 1 Sam. 1:11; Num.6: 2-8) respecting abstinence from strong drink, from the use of the razor, and from other things. Nor is there any reference to any specific passage in the Old Testament in which the word Nazareth or Nazarite or Nazarene occurs. The prophecies to which Matthew refers as being fulfilled by our Lord's making his home in the obscure unrenowned country village of Nazareth, are those which speak of His humble origin, His lowly estate, and His meek and gentle spirit, the fulfilment of which caused Nathanael to exclaim in incredulous surprise, "Can there any good thing come out of Nazareth? " (John 1: 46), and which caused the proud and haughty Pharisees to stagger in unbelief as they replied to the testimony of Nicodemus, " Search and look, for out of Galilee ariseth no prophet" (John 7:52).

It must never be forgotten that the Bible as we have it is a collection of occasional writings, flung out like sparks from the anvil upon certain definite historical occasions, every fragment, however small, containing all the essential elements and kindling properties of the Divine fire. However brief the morning or evening portion, and however imperfectly the connection with its immediate or its larger context may be apprehended, it is itself a breath of the Spirit of God, and the cumulative influence of several passages all bearing on the same topic creates an atmosphere in the human spirit and awakens an impulse in the human will, in the inspiration and the strength of which the purpose for which Holy Scripture was given is realised and fulfilled. Wherever you. taste it, the sea is salt. Wherever you dip into it, the Word of God is alive. There is a sermon in every text, life in every line, God in every word.

The writer would strongly urge the value of this method of Bible Study upon those who have no other book than the Bible. The study of this Book, chapter by chapter, and verse by verse, read in the light of the whole Bible, and interpreted in the light of the Bible as a whole, is in itself a liberal education. It was the method adopted, and constantly pursued, by the writer's own mother. She had no other book. She knew no other method. But the result of her life-long application of this method of study to the Bible was the appropriation of its essential teaching into the concrete realities of Christian character, and the transcendent peace and holy joy of a daily walk with God.

The writer has before him at this moment a copy of the Bible which is his own peculiar and sacred treasure. It was given to him by his father's aunt who died at the age of one hundred and a half years. It has been his life-long possession. On leaving his home in the country, at the age of fourteen, for the dangers and temptations, the advantages and the attractions of life in London, his mother wrote with her own hand, on the fly-leaf of this Bible, the following verses and the text of Scripture, which exactly express his own sense of the incomparable value of the Word of God

THE BIBLE

"This Holy Book I'd rather own,

Than all the gold and gems

That e'er in monarch's coffers shone,

Than all their diadems.

Nay, were the seas one chrysolite,

The earth one golden ball,

And diamonds all the stars of night,

This Book were worth them all.

Ah, no, the soul ne'er found relief,

In glittering hoards of wealth,

Gems dazzle not the eye of grief,

Gold cannot purchase health.

But here a blessed balm appears,

To heal the deepest woe,

And those who read this Book in tears,

Their tears shall cease to flow."

The hand of our God is upon all them for good that seek him; but his power and his wrath is against all them that forsake him " (Ezra 8:22).

Chapter 4 C
The Topical Method, Or Bible Study by Topics

One of the most familiar methods of handling Christian truth is for the preacher or teacher to select a subject or topic, and then find out what the Bible says, or what he himself can say, about it. Some preachers announce the topic or subject on which they propose to speak. Some times they choose topics that are not Scriptural. In all topical preaching there is a tendency to go beyond the limits of the Bible and introduce matter that is not strictly Biblical. It then ceases to be a method of Bible Study or Bible teaching at all.

In pursuing this method, it is a matter of the first importance that the Bible student should be systematic. He should make a comprehensive list of topics or subjects, so large as to include the whole range of Bible teaching. The chief peril of this method of Bible Study is the unequal emphasis which we are liable to place on certain topics which appeal to our interest, and which are too often selected for treatment, to the neglect of other topics equally important and equally prominent in Holy Scripture, which are perhaps never dealt with by us at all.

Bible Study by topics should not be casual, dealing with a single topic, only, nor should it be merely serial, as when a single group of connected topics is dealt with in serial order. It should be comprehensive, systematic, synthetic ; that is to say, an attempt should be made to cover the whole ground occupied by the entire Bible from Genesis to Revelation.

The following classification embraces all the principal kinds of topics by the study of which a knowledge of the main purport and content of the whole Bible may be obtained

1.Biographies,, e.g. the life of Abraham, Moses, Elijah, Peter, Paul.

2. Doctrines, e.g. the Atonement; the Second Advent, the work of the Holy Spirit..

3. Duties, e.g. watchfulness, hospitality, industry, forbearance, charity.

4. Places, e.g. Bethlehem, Hebron, Capernaum, Gethsemane, Calvary.

5. Events, e.g. the Exodus, the conquest of Canaan, the building of the Temple, the crucifixion of our Lord, the conversion of Saul..

6. Words, e.g. Abba, Amen, everlasting, predestinated, testimony.

7. Dispensations or methods of Divine government initiated at various epochs, and maintained throughout successive ages of the world's history, viz

(1) The dispensation of innocence, ending with the Fall, and represented by the tree of knowledge.

(2) The dispensation of conscience, ending with the Flood, and represented by Noah's Ark.

(3) The dispensation of government, authority or magistracy, ending with Abraham, and represented by the rainbow.

(4) The dispensation of promise, lasting for a period of four hundred and thirty years (Gal.3:17), ending at Sinai, and represented by Isaac.

(5) The dispensation of the Law, ending at Calvary, and represented by the tables of testimony.

(6) The dispensation of " the gospel of the grace of God," in which we are now living, which is to end with the Second Advent, and which is represented by the Cross.

(7) The dispensation of the millennium, beginning with the binding of Satan, lasting a thousand years, ending at the day of judgment, and represented by the Great White Throne.

(8) The dispensation of the Eternal Age, beginning with a new heaven and a new earth, enduring for ever and ever, and represented by the tree of life.

Good work always pays. It brings its own reward. It deepens interest. It develops a consciousness of power. It awakens a feeling of mastery. It is essential that in this method of Bible Study the student should be thorough. He should collect all the passages that bear upon the subject chosen. If the topic is that of a Scripture biography he should analyse the character, noting elements of power and weakness, success and failure, privileges and limitations, advantages. and disadvantages, mistakes made, perils avoided, and help obtained from God.

It is most important that the Bible student should be exact in all his inferences and sure of all his conclusions. He should note carefully the real sense and true meaning of each passage considered, and should neglect all merely verbal and superficial resemblances which have no real bearing on the subject in hand.

That the study should yield a profitable result, it is a prime necessity that the student should be practical. He should examine the bearing of the truths taught upon the conduct of life. He should classify his results and summarise the lessons to be learnt from them. He should ever remember that Holy Scripture was given to us by God, not merely and not chiefly to satisfy the intellect, but first and chiefly to quicken the conscience, to correct the judgment, to reinforce the will, and to direct the way of our feet. Its abiding truths have a perennial message and a present-day application to the circumstances of this, as of every other age, and to study its truths without attempting to translate them into commands bearing upon practical life, is to linger on in a realm through which it may be necessary for us to pass, but in which it is fatal for us to stay.

All Bible Study should have an object as well as a subject, and that object is not attained until the truth is applied in such a way as to awaken a response in the heart and conscience of the Bible reader, which shall bear fruit in practical conduct and daily life.

Three good books may be recommended as affording all the material that will be required for the profitable employment of this method of Bible Study.

1. Inglis's Bible Text Cyclopcedia .

This is a complete classification of Scrip- ture texts in the form of an alphabetical index of subjects. It tabulates every subject, whether doctrinal, devotional, practical, ecclesiastical, historical, biographical, or secular, which has a place in the Sacred Volume. The topics are arranged in alphabetical order, and every text belonging to each topic has been carefully collected and placed under its own appropriate head. The abstract or list of subjects at the end of the book embraces a comprehensive survey of all the essential truths of Holy Scripture. These should be taken one by one, and an attempt should be made to find out all that the Bible has to say about them.

2. Nave's Topical Bible.

This is a digest of the whole of the matter contained in Holy Scripture, classified under as many headings as there are topics or subjects dealt with in the Bible. These are arranged in alphabetical order. Where the number of passages bearing upon any important subject is

very large, these passages are printed in full. In other cases, where only a few passages are to be found, the references only are given.

3. Dr. C. I. Scofield's Reference Bible

This magnificent work has already been referred to in the previous section of this chapter on " Bible Study by Marginal References." It contains an index of all the great topics of Scripture, and a summary of the teaching of the whole Bible upon each topic.

ILLUSTRATIONS OF BIBLE BIOGRAPHIES

Reading. Topic.

I. Adam

Gen. 1. Adam created in the image of God.

Gen. 2 Adam placed in the garden of Eden.

Gen. 3. Adam's temptation and fall. ,

Job 31 Adam covered his transgression and hid his iniquity.

Rom. 5. Adam's sin made all men sinners.

1 Tim.2 Adam sinned not ignorantly but deliberately.

2. Abel

Gen. 4 Abel's birth, life, sacrifice, and death.

i John 3 Abel's works were righteous.

Heb. 11 Abel's sacrifice accepted because offered by faith.

Matt.23 Abel the first martyr.

Heb. 12 Abel's blood calls for vengeance; Christ's for pardon.

3. Abraham

Acts 7 Abraham's two calls-Ur to Haran, and Haran to Canaan.

Gen. 11 Abraham's first call-Ur to Haran.

Gen. 12 Abraham's second call-Haran to Canaan.

Gen. 13 Abraham separates from Lot, and dwells in Hebron.

Gen. 15 Abraham's sacrifice and covenant with God.

Gen. 16 Abraham marries Hagar-birth of Ishmael.

Gen. 17 Abraham's covenant with God confirmed by circumcision.

Gen. 18 Abraham entertains three angels and intercedes for Sodom.

Gen. 20 Abraham dwells at Gerar and deceives Abimelech.

Gen. 21 Abraham's heir ; Isaac born.

Gen. 22 Abraham offers his son Isaac.

Gen. 23 Abraham buries Sarah in the grave of Machpelah.

Gen. 25 Abraham's testament, age, death, and burial.

Neh. 9 Abraham's heart found faithful.

Rom. 4 Abraham's faith imputed to him for righteousness.

Gal. 3 Abraham the father of the faithful.

Heb. 11 Abraham's stupendous faith in God.

James.2 Abraham's faith bears the fruit of good works.

John 8 Abraham's children do the works of Abraham.

BIBLE DOCTRINES The Atonement

Reading. Topic.

2 Cor.5 Jesus died for all men.

Rom. 3 Christ Jesus set forth to be a propitiation.

John 1 Jesus takes away the sin of the world.

Heb. 2 Jesus tastes death for all men.

1 John 2 " He is the propitiation for our sins."

Gal.3 " Christ hath redeemed us from the curse of the law."

Mark 10 Christ " gave His life a ransom for many."

I Pet. 1 " We are redeemed .. by the precious blood of Christ."

Heb.10 Christ " offered one sacrifice for sins forever."

1 Pet.3 " Christ also hath once suffered for sins."

Is. 53 Christ bore the iniquity of us all.

Matt. 26 Christ's blood was shed for the remission of sins.

Acts 20. Christ purchased the Church with His own blood.

1 Cor.15 " Christ died for our sins according to the Scriptures."

Col. 1. In Christ " we have redemption through His blood."

III.-BIBLE DUTIES Watchfulness

Reading. Topic.

Ex. 23 " In all things be circumspect."

Ex. 34 " Take heed to thyself."

Deut. 4 " Keep thy soul diligently lest thou forget."

Deut.11 " Take heed that your heart be not deceived."

Reading. Topic.

Josh. 22 " Take diligent heed to do the commandment."

Josh. 23. "Take good heed that ye love the Lord."

Ps. 4 " Stand in awe and sin not."

Prov 4. " Keep thy heart with all diligence."

Matt. 24 " Therefore be ye also ready. '

Matt.25 " They that were ready went in with him."

Luke 12 " Take heed and beware of covetousness."

Luke 21 " Watch ye therefore and pray always."

1 Cor.3 " Let every man take heed how he buildeth."

Ephes, 5. " See that ye walk circumspectly."

1 Thess. 5. "Let us watch and be sober."

Rev. 16 " Behold, I come as a thief."

IV.-BIBLE PLACES

Bethlehem

Reading. Topic.

Gen. 48 Rachel died at Bethlehem.

Micah 5. Bethlehem the birthplace of the Ruler in Israel.

Ruth 1. Bethlehem the home of Naomi and Ruth.

Ruth 2. Bethlehem the home of Boaz.

1 Sam. 16 Bethlehem the home of David.

2 Sam. 23 The exploit of David's mighty men at Bethlehem.

Matt. 2. Bethlehem the birthplace of Christ.

V.-BIBLE EVENTS

The Conversion of Saul

Reading. Topic.

Acts 7 Saul's part in Stephen's death.

Acts 9. Saul's conversion as told by Luke.

Acts 22. Saul's conversion as told by himself to the Jews.

Acts 26. Saul's conversion as told by himself to Agrippa.

Gal. 1. Saul's conversion as told by himself to the Galatians.

1 Tim.1. Saul's conversion as told by himself to Timothy.

1 Cor. 9 Saul's conversion as referred to by himself in his Epistle to the Corinthians.

VI.-BIBLE WORDS

Amen

Reading. Topic.

Deut. 27. A strong affirmation, equivalent to an oath.

Neh. 5. A strong confirmation of the act of Nehemiah.

2 Cor. 1. A strong expression signifying firm, established, sure.

i Kings 1. A strong confirmation of the words of David.

1 Chron. 16. A strong endorsement of David's psalm by the people.

Neh. 8. A strong endorsement of the words of Ezra.

Luke 23. Our Lord's endorsement of a sinner's prayer (Verily = Amen).

1 Cor. 14. Intelligent confirmation of the words of another.

Rev. 19. A strong affirmation of the just judgment of God.

Rev. 3. One of the names of the unchanging Christ.

VII.-BIBLE DISPENSATIONS

Reading. Topic.

Gen.1 First Dispensation-Innocence, ending with the fall.

Gen. 3. Second Dispensation-Conscience, ending with the flood.

Gen. 8. Third Dispensation-Magistracy, ending with Abraham.

Gen. 12. Fourth Dispensation-Promise, ending at Sinai.

Ex. 19. Fifth Dispensation-Law, ending at Calvary.

John 1. Sixth Dispensation-Grace, ending at the Second Advent.

Rev. 20. Seventh Dispensation-The millennium,ending at the Great White Throne.

Rev. 21. Eighth Dispensation-The eternal age of the New Heaven and the New Earth, which has no end, but endures for ever and ever.

Chapter 4 D
The Typical Method, Or Bible Study by Types

It is not good to despise any part of Scripture, least of all such parts as are directly related to Jesus Christ.

It is our great misfortune that the study of the types has fallen on evil times, and that as a method of Bible Study it has almost ceased to be taught or used. It is even treated with contempt, and there are books on Bible Study in which the attempt to trace the hidden spiritual meaning and intention of the regulations of the Tabernacle worship is denounced as a " riot of undisciplined thinking." The censure is perhaps deserved by some writers who have put forward their own extravagant fancies in place of the sober and restrained teaching. of the Bible itself ; but the abuse of a method is no argument against the right and proper use of it, and the first result of the revival of a rational systematic study of the types will be to enforce the exclusion of all these inventions of mere human fancy, and to demand a definite Scripture warrant for every type that is taught.

The study of the types is the only method of entering into the real and primary meaning of large portions of Holy Scripture. The Temple is a mere shambles, and the books of Exodus and Leviticus are sealed books to those who have no insight into the types. But to those who would enter into the true intent and purpose of these books, and gather from them the mind of the Spirit, they are fragrant of Christ in every verse, and full of grace and truth in every line.

It was entirely agreeable to man's nature, as a being compounded of body as well as soul, that God should represent spiritual things by means of sensible things, and it was particularly well adapted to the needs of God's people in the infancy or non-age of the Church. Nevertheless, there is need for the study of the types in the present day, in order that the people of God may obtain clearer and more vivid insight into all the wealth of Gospel truth, and into the whole mystery and glory of the grace of Christ.

A consideration of the words used in Scripture to express a type will show how extensively the system of what we may call kindergarten instruction, or teaching by types, pervades the Old Testament, and how fully this method is employed in the interpretation of the Old Testament by the writers of the New Testament.Eight words are used to express the nature of a type

(i) The word type itself is used in John 20: 25: " Except I shall see in His hands the type (print) of the nails, and put my finger into the type (print) of. the nails, and thrust my hand into His side, I will not believe." This verse gives us the clue to the meaning of the word. As the hole corresponds- in size and shape, and in other respects is an exact counterpart to the nail which makes it, so the type corresponds to the, antitype, or the reality of which it is the type.

(2) The word shadow is. used in Col.2: I6, 17: " Let no man therefore judge you in meat, or in drink, or in respect of an holy day, or of the new moon, or of the Sabbath days : which are a shadow of things to come."

(3) The word example is used in Hebrews 8: 4, 5 : " There are priests that offer gifts according to the law : who serve unto the example and shadow of heavenly things, as Moses was admonished of God when he was about to make the tabernacle."

(4) The word sign is used in Matthew 12: 39: " An evil and adulterous generation seeketh after a sign ; and there shall no sign be given to it, but the sign of the 'prophet Jonas."

(5) The word figure is used in Hebrews 11:19 : " From whence also he received him in a figure."

(6) The word allegory is used in Galatians 4: 24: " Which things are an allegory."

(7) The word seal is used in Romans 4: 11 : " And he received the sign of circumcision, a seal of the righteousness' of the faith which he had being yet uncircumcised."

(8) The word letter is used in 2 Corinthians 3: 6. " The letter (i.e. the law) killeth, but the spirit (i.e. the gospel) quickeneth."

Similarly eight words are used to express the nature of the antitype or reality to which the type corresponds, and which it prefigures or shadows forth:

(1) The word antitype itself is used in 1 Peter 3: 21: . "The like antitype (figure) whereunto even baptism doth also now save us."

(2) The word body is used in Colossians 2:17: "Which are a shadow of things to come ; but the body is of Christ."

(3) The words very image are used in Hebrews 10:1: " For the law having a shadow of good things to come, and not the very image of the things, can never with those sacrifices which they offered year by year continually make the comers thereunto perfect."

(4) The words good things to come are used in Hebrews 10:1 : "The law having a shadow of good :things to come."

(5) The words things in the heavens are used in Hebrews 9:23: " It was necessary therefore that the patterns of things in the heavens should be purified with these."

(6) The words the true are used in Hebrews 9: 24: "For Christ is not entered into the holy places made with hands, which are the figures of the true."

(7) The word spirit is used in 2 Corinthians 3: 6 : " For the letter killeth but the spirit quickeneth."

(8) The word spiritually is used in Revelation 11: 8 : " The great city, which spiritually is called Sodom and Egypt, where also our Lord was crucified."

It will greatly assist us in this study if we have a clear definition of what is meant by a type, and this is given us in Scripture itself. A type is " a shadow of good things to come" (Hebrews 10:10). A type involves three things (i) an outward sensible object or thing which represents some other higher thing; (2) that other higher thing represented, which we call the antitype or the reality and (3) the work of the type which is expressed in the term " representing " or " shadowing forth." A type is a sign, a resemblance, a pattern, a figure, a shadow. As a parable is an earthly story with a heavenly meaning, so a type is an outward and visible earthly thing by which God has designed to teach us some invisible, spiritual, heavenly thing. A type is some outward and sensible thing ordained of God under the Old Testament to hold forth something of Christ or something in relation to Him in the New Testament. The type is the shadow, the antitype is the substance ; the type is the shell, the antitype is the kernel ; the type is the letter or the law, the antitype is the spirit or the gospel. The work of the type is to adumbrate-or shadow forth something of Christ and His benefits.

It will be well for us to draw a clear distinction between types on the one hand and similes, parables, ceremonies, and sacraments on the other.

A type is a divinely instituted resemblance.

A simile is an arbitrary comparison or natural illustration. Marriage is a comparison setting forth the mystic union of Christ and the Church ; but it is not a type, for it was instituted for another purpose. It is a sign but not a sacrament. In the parable of the Marriage Supper, the bread is only a similitude. In the sacrament of the Lord's Supper, it is designed and set apart to represent Christ, and is therefore typical.

A parable is a similitude which has God for its author, but it is not a type, for God does not set the stamp of institution upon it and make it an ordinance.

A ceremony is always a type, but a type is not always a ceremony. The pillar of cloud and fire was a type but not a ceremony. A ceremony was a law or an observance prescribed to teach some gospel mystery.

A sacrament differs from a type in two ways. There are many types, but there are only two Sacraments-Baptism and the Lord's Supper. In nature they differ only in this : types are the signs of Christ coming-sacraments are the signs of Christ already come.

The following four rules for the understanding of the types of the Old Testament are taken from Samuel Mather's Figures or Types of the Old Testament," the great standard work on this subject. They embody all that it is necessary for the beginner to know in order to prosecute the method of Bible Study by types with rich and fruitful and fascinating results.

Rule i.-God is the only Author of the type.

That which the type bears of likeness to Christ is stamped and engraven upon it by Divine institution. A type is not a mere natural similitude or resemblance which may be chosen arbitrarily and used by way of illustration by anyone. As the Church in the New Testament has no power to make sacraments, so they of the Old Testament had no power to make types. It is of the essence of a type that it should be divinely instituted, and set apart by God, for the express purpose of setting before us something of Christ.

We cannot safely say that anything is a type unless we have Scripture warrant for it. It is the error of allowing fancy and imagination to run riot in the matter of the types which has brought the whole study into disrepute.

Scripture warrant for regarding anything as a type is given in three forms.

(1) By express statement, e.g. Adam was "the figure of Him that was to come" (Rom. 5:14). " The law was a shadow of good things to come" (Heb.10:1). The land of Canaan was a figure of " a better country, that is a heavenly." (Heb.11:16).

(2) By permutation, or change of names between the type and the antitype, e.g. when Christ is called David (Ezekiel 34: 23), or Adam (1 Cor. 15:45), or the Lamb of God (John 1: 29), or our Passover (1 Cor. 5:7) ; or when Moses is called a mediator (Gal.3:19), or a sheep is called a sacrifice, or is said to make - atonement, or to expiate sin, there being in truth but one Mediator, one Sacrifice, one Atonement, and one Expiation, of which Moses and the victims offered on the altar are but types.

(3) Where there is a clear and evident analogy and parallel between things under the law and things under the Gospel, enabling us to conclude that such legal dispensations were intended and given by God as types of the Gospel mysteries whose image they bear. Thus Joseph may be looked upon as a type of Christ, though Scripture nowhere expressly calls him such, and the deliverance out of Egypt may be regarded as a type of the deliverance of the Church from the bondage of sin. The analogy is so clear that we may justly infer that God intended the one to be a type of the other. But we must not indulge in our fancy and make anything a type unless we have Scripture ground for it. The constitution of the type, like every other method of Revelation, is the prerogative of God and God alone.

Rule 2.-Types are not only signs but seals.

As signs they shadow forth, but as seals they pledge and make sure the benefits of Christ to which they are related. Abraham received the sign of circumcision, a seal of the righteousness of faith (Rom. 4:11). If they were signs at all, then they were more than signs, for if they signified to our intellect what the Messiah would be, they at the same time assured our faith that the Messiah certainly would be that which the type signified.

Rule 3.-The types relate not only to the Person of Christ but also to all His benefits, to all Gospel truths and mysteries, and even to our miseries without Christ.

Thus Circumcision is a type of Baptism. The Passover is a type of the Lord's Supper. Leprosy is a type of our natural pollution through sin. Hagar and Ishmael are types of the Covenant of Works. Doeg and Ahithophel are types of Judas. Gehenna or the Valley of Hinnom is a type of Hell.

Rule 4.-As there is always a similitude and an analogy in something, so there is ever a dissimilitude and a disparity between the type and the antitype in certain other things.

Adam is a type of Christ, but the second Adam infinitely transcends the first. Some types are partial and represent Christ in one particular only, as Jonah, who foreshadowed Christ in the one thing of His abiding in the grave for three days and rising again : David is sometimes called a total type of Christ, because he resembled Him in so many points; but no type can be called total, certainly not David, for he was only prophet and king, whereas Christ is Prophet, Priest, and King.

The following books may be recommended as helpful to those who propose to undertake a course of Bible Study by types.

(1) " The Study of the Types," by Ada Habershon (Morgan & Scott.) is a convenient and a comprehensive little text-book on the subject.

(2) C.H.MacKintosh's "Notes on the Pentateuch: Genesis to Deuteronomy " (Loizeaux Bros. Inc) are a perfect gold-mine to those capable of appreciating the wealth of spiritual teaching contained in Scripture types. But there is nothing to compare with

(3) Samuel Mather's " Figures or Types of the Old Testament" (published in 1705, and now out of print, but sometimes obtainable second-hand), from which the principal contents of this section are drawn.

The following classification embraces all the principal kinds of sensible objects or things selected and used in Holy Scripture, as types representing or shadowing forth corresponding spiritual realities:

1. Individual persons, e.g. Adam.

2. Orders of persons, e.g. priests.

3. Actions, viz. deliverances and destructions, e.g. the passage of Israel through the Red Sea.

4. Things, e.g. Jacob's ladder.

5. The institutions of the ceremonial law, e.g. circumcision.

6. Holy places, e.g. the burning bush.

7. The Tabernacle and the Temple.

ILLUSTRATIONS

I.-INDIVIDUAL PERSONS

Reading. Topic.

Rom. 5 Adam, a type of Christ, the head of a new race.

I Thess. 4 Epoch, a type of Christ's ascension, and a pledge of ours.

1 Pet.3 Noah, a type of Christ preaching and saving believers.

Heb. 7 Melchizedek, a type of 'the eternal priesthood of Christ.

Gen.22. Abraham, a type of Christ's absolute obedience to God.

Heb. 11. Isaac, a type of Christ's miraculous birth.

Gen. 32. Jacob, a type of Christ's sojourning and wrestling.

Ps. 105. Joseph, a type of Christ in suffering and exaltation.

Exod. 3 Moses, a type of Christ delivering us from bondage.

Josh. 1. Joshua, a type of Christ bringing us into rest.

Judges 16. Samson, a type of Christ in strength, suffering, and death.

2 Sam 8 David, a type of Christ in his conquests and victories

1 Kings 4 Solomon, a type of Christ in wisdom and world-wide dominion.

Matt. 17. Elijah, a type of John the Baptist, the forerunner.

2 Kings 2 Elisha, a type of Christ continuing with His people.

Matt. 12. Jonah, a type of Christ's death, burial, and resurrection.

Ezra 5 Zerubbabel, a type of Christ leading out of captivity.

Zech. 3. Joshua the high priest, a type of Christ restoring purity of worship.

II.-ORDER OF PERSONS

Reading. Topic.

Is. 49. The Jewish nation, a type of Christ who is called Israel

Gal. 6 The Jewish nation a type of the Church which is also called Israel.

Rom.8 The first-born, a type of Christ : " the firstborn among many brethren."

Heb. 12. The first-born, a type of "the Church of the first-born."

Num. 6 The Nazarite, a type of Christ, separated unto God.

1 Pet. 2. The Nazarite, a type of the Church, a holy people.

Deut. 18. Prophets, types of Christ, who taught the will of God.

I Cor 14. Prophets, types of the Church, with its gift of prophecy.

Heb. 5 Priests, types of Christ, our great High Priest.

Rev. 1. Priests, types of the Christian, a priest unto God.

Ps. 2 Kings, types of Christ in their authority.

2 Sam.7 Kings, types of Christ in their perpetuity.

Ps. 72. Kings, types of Christ in their executive activity.

III.-ACTIONS, viz. DELIVERANCES AND DESTRUCTIONS

Readings. Topic.

Ex. 12. Deliverance out of Egypt, a, type of our

Ps. 105. deliverance out of the spiritual bondage and misery of sin.

Ex. 14. and 15. The passage of the Red Sea a type of our deliverance from the relentless pursuit of spiritual foes.

Deut. 1. and Ps. 95 The march through the wilderness, a type of the earthly pilgrimage of this present life.

Josh. 3 and 4 The passage of the Jordan, a type of Christ going before His people through the waters of death.

Deut. 11. and Josh 5 Entrance into Canaan, a type of Christ introducing His people to the rest of the promised land.

Is. 35 and 40. Deliverance out of Babylon, a type of the destruction of the yoke of the world.

2 Pet. 2 and Jude. Destruction of Sodom, a type of all unnatural lusts and uncleanness.

Ezek. 30. and Rev.11 Destruction of Egypt, a type of all idolatry, oppression and cruelty.

Josh. 6 and I Kings 16. Destruction of Jericho, a type of the irreparable ruin of those who fight against God.

Jer. 49. and Obad. Destruction of Edom, a type of implacable hatred toward the people of God.

Jer. l. and Rev. 18. Destruction of Babylon, a type of the destruction of the enemies of the Gospel.

Jer. 7 and 19. Tophet and Gehenna (The Valley of Hinnom), a type of hell.

IV.-THINGS

Reading. Topic.

Gen. 28. Jacob's ladder, a type of Christ connecting heaven and earth.

Exod.3 The burning bush, a type of the Church ,persecuted yet preserved.

Num. 9. The pillar of cloud and fire, a type Christ's perpetual presence.

John 6 Manna, a type of Christ, the Bread of Life.

1 Cor. 10 The smitten rock, a type of Christ, the Water of Life.

Num. 21. The brazen serpent, a type of Christ lifted up on the Cross, in order to save.

John 5 The waters of Bethesda, a type of Christ's healing power.

V.-THE INSTITUTIONS OF THE CEREMONIAL LAW

Reading. Topic.

Gen. 17. Circumcision, a seal of admission to the Covenant.

Mark 16. Circumcision, a figure of baptism, the initiatory rite of the Church.

Lev. 1. Sacrifices-the burnt-offering, a type of obedience.

Lev. 2. Sacrifices-the meal offering, a type of service.

Lev. 3. Sacrifices-the peace offering, a type of fellowship.

Lev. 4. Sacrifices-the sin Offering, a type of expiation.

Lev. 5 Sacrifices-the trespass offering, a type of restitution.

Lev. 6. Sacrifices-the consecration offering, a type of separation unto God.

Heb. 9. Purifications-cleanings, ceremonial and spiritual.

Lev. 23: 4-14. Festivals-The Feast of the Passover Redemption.

Lev.23: 15-21. Festivals —The Feast of Pentecost-The Holy Spirit.

Lev.23: 33-34. Festivals-The Feast of Tabernacles-Incarnation.

Num. 29. Festivals-The Feast of Trumpets-the sound of the Gospel.

Lev. 16. Festivals-The Day of Afonement-the expiation of sin.

Ezek. 46, Festivals-The New Moon-a solemn assembly.

Exod. 31. Festivals-Sabbaths-the seventh day, a day of rest.

Deut. 15. Festivals-Sabbaths-the seventh year, a year of release from debt.

Lev. 25. Festivals—Sabbaths-the year of jubilee, a year of release from slavery.

VI.-HOLY PLACES

Reading. Topic.

Acts 7 The burning bush-holy ground.

Josh. 5. The place where God appeared to Joshua holy ground.

Exod. 19. Mount Sinai-the holy mount.

2 Pet. 1. The mount of transfiguration-the holy mount.

Zech. 2. The land of Canaan-the holy land.

Josh. 20. Cities of Refuge-holy places of refuge.

Ps. 48. Jerusalem-the holy city.

VII-THE TABERNACLE AND THE TEMPLE Reading.

Topic.

Exod. 38. The altar of burnt-offering-atonement.

2 Chron. 4 The molten sea and lavers-cleansing.

Exod. 30. The altar of incense-prayer.

Exod. 25. 31-40 The golden candlestick-the Light of theWorld.

Exod. 25. 23-30 The table a of shew-bread-the Bread of Life.

1 Chron. 13. The ark of the covenant, with the cherubim, the Shekinah light, the mercy-seat, the tables of the law, the pot of manna,- and Aaron's rod-Divine G

VIII.-SAMUEL MATHER'S CLASSIFICATION OF THE TYPES

Types

I. Personal

1. Individual persons:

(1) Before the law-Adam, Enoch, Noah, Melchizedek, Abraham, Isaac, Jacob, Joseph.

(2) Under the law- Moses, Joshua, Samson, David, Solomon, Elijah, Elisha, Jonah Zerubbael, Joshua the priest:

2. Typical orders of persons

(1) Jewish nation.

(2) First-born.

(3) Nazarites.

(4) Prophets.

(5) Priests. Kings.

II. Real

1.Occasional

(i) Things-Jacob's ladder.

Moses' burning bush.

Pillar of cloud and fire.

Manna.

The Rock.

Brazen serpent.

Waters of Bethesda.

(2) Actions-

i. Deliverances of God's people:

(i.) Deliverance out of Egypt.

(ii.) Passage through the sea.

(iii.) March through the wilderness.

(iv.) Passage through Jordan.

(v) Entrance into Canaan.

(vi.) Deliverance out of Babylon.

ii. Destruction of enemies

(i.) Sodom, Egypt, Jericho, Edam, and Babylon-types of Rome.

(ii.) The Deluge, Sodom, Egypt, and Tophet-types of Hell.

2. Perpetual, the ceremonial law

I. Circumcision

1. Sign or external part.

2. Mystery or what covenant it relates to.

(I) Not to the covenant of works.

(2) To the covenant of Grace implying

i. To be a God to Abraham.

ii. To give him a seed.

(i.) Great seed, Messiah.

(ii.) A church seed.

(iii. Believing Jewish seed.

(iv.) Ingrafted Gentile seed.

iii. To provide an inheritance.

3. What respect it has to this covenant.

1.As a seal

2 As holding forth Christ's sufferings.

3 Especially Christ's righteousness.

4 It respected mortification.

5.It shadowed forth baptism.

II. Sacrifices

I. Burnt-offering (I) of the Herd (2) of the Flock (3) of Fowls.

2. Meat offering.

3. Peace offering.

4. Sin offering.

5.Trespass offering.

6. Consecration offering.

III. Purifications, whence consider

1. Ceremonial uncleanness by

(1) Unclean eating and

touchings

(2) Unclean issues.

(3) Leprosy.

2. Ceremonial cleansings from

(1) Unclean eating and touchings.

(2) Unclean issues.

(3) Leprosy.

3.How ceremonial cleansing typified spiritual cleansing.

IV. Festivals

1. Feasts-Passover, Pentecost, Tabernacles, Trumpets, Expiation.

2. New Moons.

3. Sabbaths-Seventh Day, Seventh Year, Fiftieth Year or Jubilee.

V. Temple Officers

I. Kinds-Priests, Levites, Nethinims.

(1) What they typified-Christ, His ministers, His members.

(2) Wherein they were types-In their personal qualifications, apparel, consecration, ministration or work.

2. Maintenance.

VI. Holy Places

Holy Places

I. Transient

1. Burning bush or place of God's appearing to Moses.

2. Place where God appeared to Joshua.

3. Mount Sinai.

4. Mount of Christ's Transfiguration.

II. Permanent, during the Jewish economy.

1. Land of Canaan,.

2. Cities of Refuge.

3. Tabernacle and Temple-Builders, time, place, materials,parts, viz.

(1) House- 1.. Common Parts - Foundation, walls, doors, windows floor, roof.

ii. Special Parts-porch, sanctuary, oracle, chambers.

(2) Courts- Outward, inward.

(3) Vessels-

1. Of natural necessity.

ii. Typical and instituted.

(i.) Without of brass-Two pillars, altar of burnt-offering, molten sea and lavers

(ii.) Within of gold_

In the Sanctuary - Candlestick, shew-bread table.

In the Holy of Holies-Vessels for offering incense, the Ark with its appurtenances.

Chapter 4 E

The Cyclopaedic Method, Or Bible Study by Bible Dictionary

We have now dealt with the four primary methods of Bible Study-the Synthetic, the Parallel, the Topical, and the Typical. In a sense it may be said that there are these four methods of Bible Study and these four only, for the remaining three methods are concerned with the use of books of reference of three different kinds. In these three books of reference, the knowledge gained by the application of the foregoing methods is gathered up and placed together in such a form as to be available for immediate use in reference to any particular topic, any single word, or any consecutive portion of Scripture in the study of which the Bible reader is occupied.

The remaining three methods of Bible Study are therefore secondary and subsidiary, and are intended to facilitate the use of the first four methods by rendering available the results of the labours and researches of other investigators and students of the Word.

The cyclopaedic method of Bible Study by Bible dictionary is closely allied to the topical method of Bible Study by topics. The microscopic method of Bible Study by concordance is closely allied to the parallell method of Bible Study by marginal references. The explanatory method of Bible Study by commentary gathers up the results of all previous study and research, and arranges it in order, consecutively, book by book, chapter by chapter, and verse by verse, from Genesis to Revelation, under the text which the comment is designed to explain.

The cyclopaedic method of Bible Study by Bible dictionary consists in the exhaustive study of all the proper names and all the principal, topics of Holy Scripture. Every good Bible dictionary contains an article on every place and every person, on every book and every doctrine dealt with in the Bible. The cyclopaedic method embraces the study of nouns or names, of the great substantives, persons, places, and things mentioned in the Bible.

The writer always recommends Fausset's " Critical and Expository Bible Cyclopaedia." It is one of the best as well as one of the cheapest. It was formerly published by Hodder & Stoughton.. It is a large book well worth the original price.

The idea of the Bible dictionary is to bring together in a single article all that is known about some one person, place, or thing mentioned in Scripture ; and since we know, in most cases, very little more than what is told us in Scripture itself about these persons, places, and things, .a Bible dictionary is practically a collection of all that is contained in the Bible put together under the various headings of the particular subjects treated of, these being arranged in alphabetical order.

A glance at the titles of the articles in Fausset's " Bible Cyclopaedia " will enable us to classify all the more important contributions under a little over a dozen headings.

1. Persons, e.g. Abraham.

2. Places, e.g. Hebron.

3. Animals, e.g. adder.

4. Vegetables, e.g. almond tree.

5. Minerals, e.g. amethyst.

6. Peculiar words, e.g. anathema.

7. Peculiar things, e.g. habergeon.

8. Arts, e.g. agriculture.

9. Institutions, e.g. Passover.

10. Doctrines, e.g. atonement.

11. Practices, e.g. baptism.

12. Customs, e.g. calf-worship.

13. Books of the Bible, e.g. Genesis.

14. Archaeological articles, e.g. Egypt.

15. Theological articles, e.g. Holy Ghost.

The trend of Fausset is toward a reasonable, scholarly, evangelical interpretation of the Scriptures, and against modem rationalistic tendencies, the errors of which are frequently exposed. All branches of study, including natural history, classic literature, and modern discoveries, are laid under contribution, as far as they help to elucidate the meaning of the Word of God.

Chapter 4 F

The Microscopic Method, Or Bible Study by Concordance

The microscopic method, or Bible Study by concordance, is an extension of the parallel method of Bible Study by marginal references, only, instead of giving us some of the references to other passages of Scripture in which the subject of the text is dealt with, as in the case of marginal references, the concordance gives us all the references to all the other passages of Scripture in which every word in the text is found.

The purposes for which we turn to the pages of a good concordance are these

(1) To find the place in which a word or a passage occurs.

(2) To obtain a list of all the occurrences of that word.

(3) To obtain a knowledge of the exact force and the exact shade of meaning conveyed by the original Hebrew or Greek word which the English word in the passage translates.

The writer recommends Strong's " Exhaustive Concordance," published by Hodder & Stoughton , but if anyone already has Young's "Analytical Concordance," that also is an excellent work, arranged on a different principle, but perhaps equally useful, and certainly sufficient for all practical purposes. Personally the writer has both, and would not on any account be without either. For those who wish to follow up more closely the meaning of the Hebrew and Greek originals, without having the advantage of any knowledge whatever of these languages, the writer recommends The Englishman's Hebrew and Chaldee Concordance to the Old Testament," and " The Englishman's Greek Concordance to the New Testament," but these are expensive works. Strong's " Exhaustive Concordance " consists of eight parts. It is necessary to read the preface in order to know how to use it. It is a concordance to the original Greek and Hebrew Scriptures in English, a concordance to the A.V., and a concordance to the R.V. all in one. Its treatment of the subject is, as its name indicates, exhaustive. It gives every word, including every "a" and every "the" in the Bible, and all the passages in which every word occurs. It is so complete and so perfect that it can never be superseded.

Part 1. Main Concordance

Here every word in the Bible, except those in Part 3, is found arranged in alphabetical order, and under each word is given a list of all the passages in which it occurs, with one line of the verse containing it.

Part 2. Addenda This in unimportant.

Part 3. Appendix to the Main Concordance

This gives every passage in which forty-seven little words like " a," " the," " and," " as," " for," "he," "she," " it," etc., occur.

Part 4. Comparative Concordance

This is a concordance to the R.V., exhibiting every instance in which it differs from the A.V., and from the version of the American Revision Committee, of which the author, James Strong, LL.D., was a member. An asterisk (*) indicates a change from the Authorised Version (A.V.) in both the British Revised Version (R.V.) and the American Revised Version (A.R.V.). An obelisk (t) indicates a change in the R.V. only. A double obelisk (tt) indicates a change in the A.R.V. only.

Part 5. Notanda

Though short this is very interesting. It is a list of all the one hundred and forty-three longer passages in which important changes have been made in the R.V. and the A.R.V., as compared with the A.V.

Part 6. Addenda -Unimportant.

Part 7. Hebrew and Chaldee Dictionary

This contains every Hebrew word in the Hebrew Bible, and gives the exact shade of its force and meaning. For the benefit of those who do not understand Hebrew the eight thousand six hundred and seventy-four words in the Hebrew Old Testament are numbered.

The number of the Hebrew word is given in the Main Concordance. By turning to the number given in the Hebrew and Chaldee Dictionary, we can ascertain the exact meaning of the original, without knowing a single word of the Hebrew language, or even a single letter of the Hebrew alphabet. At the end of Part 7 there is a list of the places where the chapters and verses are divided differently in the Hebrew from the way in which they are divided in the Authorised Version.

Part 8. Greek Dictionary of the New Testament This contains every word in the Greek New Testament, and gives the exact shade of its force and meaning. For the benefit of those who do not understand Greek, the five thousand six hundred and twenty-four words in the Greek New Testament are numbered, and to distinguish them from the words of the Hebrew Old Testament the numbers of the words in the Greek New Testament are printed in italics. The number of the Greek word is given in the Main Concordance, where of course it is again printed in italics. By turning to the number given in the Greek dictionary we can ascertain the exact meaning of the original, without knowing a single word of the Greek language or a single letter of the Greek alphabet.

As an illustration of the method of using the concordance, we may take the word " interpretation." From the Main Concordance we see that the word occurs thirty-eight times in the Old Testament, where it translates five different Hebrew words, and eight times in the New Testament, where it translates five different Greek words. By turning to the Hebrew dictionary and finding the numbers given in ordinary type, we get the exact force of the original Hebrew words translated in the thirty-eight passages of the Old Testament in which the word " interpretation " occurs ; and by turning to the Greek dictionary and finding the numbers given in italics, we get the exact force of the original Greek words translated in the eight passages of the New Testament in which the word "interpretation" occurs.. This feature renders Strong's " Concordance" a Hebrew and a Greek as well as an English concordance, available for the use of the Bible student who knows neither Hebrew nor Greek.

An anonymous English writer has made a microscopic analysis of all the books, chapters,.verses, words, and letters of the English Bible and the Apocrypha. The results are given in Dr. James Townley's "Introduction to the Literary History of the Bible." They are based on an earlier massoretical analysis, and the author is said to have spent three years of his life in making the calculations necessary for its completion.

1. The Whole Bible

Old Testament New Testament Total

Books ... 39 27 66

Chapters ...929 260 1,189

Verses ... 23,214 7,959 31,173

Words 592,439 181,253 773,692

Letters 2,728,100 838,380 3,566,480

In the Apocrypha there are 14 books, 183 chapters, 6681 verses, and 152,185 letters.

The middle chapter and the least in the whole Bible is Ps. 117.

The middle verse is Ps. 118: 8.

2. The Old Testament

The middle book of the Old Testament is Proverbs.

The middle chapter is Job 29.

The middle verse would be 1 Chronicles 29:17 if there were a verse more, and 1 Chronicles 29:18 if there were a verse less.

The shortest verse is 1 Chronicles 1: 25.

The word Jehovah occurs 6,855 times.

The word " and " occurs 35,543 times.

The verse Ezra 7:21 contains all the letters of the English alphabet.

The verse Zephaniah 3:8 contains all the letters of the Hebrew alphabet.

2 Kings 19 identical with Isaiah 37

3. The New Testament

The middle book of the New Testament is 2 Thessalonians.

The middle chapter would be Romans 13 if there were a chapter more, or Romans 14 if there were a chapter less.

The middle verse is Acts 17:17.

The shortest verse is John 11:35.

The word " and " occurs 10,684 times.

Chapter 4 G

The Explanatory Method, Or Bible Study by Commentary

Like the Bible dictionary and the Bible concordance, the Bible commentary is a work of reference. It gathers up the results of Bible Study in all other departments, and arranges the information thus obtained under the particular chapter and verse commented on.

Of Bible commentaries the number is legion. The best detailed description of all the commentaries on Holy Scripture that have been published in the English language is that given in C. H. Spurgeon's lectures entitled " Commenting and Commentaries."

For all practical purposes the present writer regards Ellicott's " Commentary on the Old and New Testaments for English Readers " (published by Cassell & Co., 8 vols.) as the best. Every Bible student and every Christian family should have at least one complete commentary on the whole Bible in the house, so as to be able to look up the meaning of any passage whenever a difficulty arises or a question is asked. The writer has been asked for the explanation of many difficult passages in the course of a lengthened experience of the study and the teaching of the Word, and he has never yet had a case in which the difficulty has not been honestly faced and suitably dealt with by Ellicott, whether the problem has always been solved or not.

The purpose of the Bible commentary is threefold: (1) to set forth the inner life and spiritual content and meaning of Scripture in such a way as to get that spiritual momentum into the heart and soul of the Bible reader ; (2) to give the exact historical situation involved in the passage of Scripture commented on ; (3) to explain dark passages and remove difficulties scientific, historical, and moral.

Ellicott gives an introduction to each book in the Bible, setting down what is known respecting the writer, the readers, the time when it - was written, the place where it was written, and the character, content and canonicity of each book. There is also frequently, and wherever necessary, an excursus on difficult subjects, e.g. the names Elohim and Jehovah, Elam and Chedorlaomer, the angel of the Lord, the chronology of the life of Jacob, etc.

The general trend and spirit of the commentary is strongly evangelical, but some of the contributors are distinctly "broad." The scholarship is ripe and modern, a combination which it is hard to find in these days without some considerable infusion of the noxious ingredients of modern doubt. It does not, like Dummelow's " Commentary on the Whole Bible," adopt the moderate, nor does it, like "The Century Bible," adopt the extreme rationalistic conclusions of the higher critics; but some few of the contributors are not so loyal to the old evangelical conception of Holy Scripture as Bishop Ellicott himself, and nearly all the other members, of his staff.

Chapter 5
How to Master the Bible

THERE are certain maxims which are applicable not only to the subject of Bible Study but also to every other form of human endeavour. The secret of success in every department of life is hard work. The man who wants to have a competent knowledge of his Bible must be prepared to work hard at it. Lightly come, lightly go ; but for real value and permanent worth there must be steady and sustained effort, and the results accruing will always be in proportion to the sacrifices made, the pains taken, and the industry displayed.

Nothing can come out of nothing. A man does not learn a language, or gain the power to play the violin, or to command a ship, without a considerable amount of steady, honest, faithful, plodding work. It is the same with Bible Study. It begins with drudgery, but by and by drudgery leads to mastery, and with the sense of mastery comes a consciousness of power which turns the drudgery into a delight.

The point at which a piece of hard work ceases to be irksome, and becomes a source of pleasure, is the point of mastery. The thing that creates interest and brings satisfaction to the worker in every department of toil and study is efficiency, and for the attainment of efficiency there must be some knowledge and some application of the methods that lead to mastery.

We are not all gifted in the same way, but everybody can do something well, and the mastery of the content of the English Bible is one of those things that lies within the compass of all. We need not envy the gifts of others. We are not all D. L. Moodys, or Campbell Morgans, or F. B. Meyers, but even " unlearned and ignorant men " have the capacity to make themselves masters here. Everybody can read the Bible. Everybody can understand it; Everybody can attain to some measure of usefulness, if not of distinction, in imparting the truths it contains to others. This is the justification of the calling of the lay-preacher and the Sunday School teacher who have been denied the inestimable advantage of a university education or a complete course of college training.

The subject lies within the reach of the ordinary wage-earning working man, and there is no occupation which yields a bigger return, in the way of intellectual interest and spiritual enjoyment, than that of Bible Study.

Everything counts and counts for ever. The mind is interested, enriched, and ennobled by a course of consecutive Bible Study, and the benefits, which such a course of study confers are not merely permanent, they are eternal.

For the mastery of the English Bible the foregoing methods of Bible Study are strongly recommended, but especially, the synthetic method of Bible Study by books. The Bible is well worthy of systematic, comprehensive, consecutive study, and any pains taken in attempting to master its content will be amply rewarded. The main thing is to read the Bible itself, not merely books on the Bible ; to read it copiously, continuously, consecutively, repeatedly, independently, and prayerfully, getting our own interpretation of its meaning and purport direct from the Holy Spirit, the Author, the inspirer, and the only true Interpreter of the written Word of God. The Bible is a supernatural Book, and it can only be mastered by supernatural aid.

Therefore let the reading of the Bible be punctuated with prayer.

The complete mastery of the content of the whole Bible, and of every book in it, is a matter that takes time ; but no better investment of time can be made, for what we sow in time we shall reap in eternity. But even apart from the harvest of eternity, there is no occupation which yields so rich a return of real enjoyment and pure pleasure as the study of the Word of God, provided that this study is undertaken in order to satisfy the soul's desire for God. We must not study the Book of Books merely as a means of gratifying our scientific and literary tastes and ambitions, or for the sake of satisfying our own intellectual curiosity. The Book was written for the purpose of introducing us to a Person, to One Who is alive, and Who is, if we only knew it, the very heart of our heart, the very life of our life. If we read it in order to find our way to Him, the result will be a renewal of the soul's interest in the life of fellowship with God, the life of personal holiness, of believing prayer, of active Christian service, and abundant missionary endeavour.

" Break Thou the Bread of Life, Dear Lord, to me,

As Thou didst break the loaves Beside the sea.

Beyond the sacred page I seek Thee, Lord;

My spirit pants for Thee,

O Living Word."

Make the best of your second best. If your time is limited and your obligations and claims in other directions are heavy, do not fail to give to Bible Study the limited amount of time and strength that you can spare for this purpose.

Go on bettering your very best. The riches of Bible truth are inexhaustible. The more we read and study the Book the more convinced we are that " the Lord hath yet more light and truth to break forth from His Word."

Chapter 6
How to Wield the Bible

ONE of the quaintest, most pertinent, and most valuable homiletic counsels ever given to a preacher of the Gospel is that contained in the maxim, "Get full of your subject, pull out the bung, and let nature caper."

Whatever may be the subject of discourse, when a man is full of it, when he is wrapped up in it, when it lies very near to his heart, when he dwells upon it day and night and can think of nothing else, he .has only to open his mouth and it will, flow liquid gold. The subject is revolved over and over in his own mind, he is acquainted with it in every aspect, it opens out before him of its own accord, he knows his way through it, and at every turn it gleams and corruscates with illustrations which do not need to be hunted for, but which present themselves in numerous and sparkling array in response to the warmth of his interest in the subject he seeks to expound.

This is true in a special degree of the study of the Bible. Once we have attained to a thorough mastery of the content of the Bible, once we succeed in getting " full of it," we shall be on the look-out for opportunities of conveying to others the truths we have learned to prize for ourselves. There is all the difference in the world between " having to say something " and " having something to say." The man who knows his Bible is never at a loss for a theme. When his heart warms to it, the subject divides itself up in his mind, and he has only to let himself go, and the inspired Word will rush through his inspired lips, or seek an outlet through his inspired pen. " Get full of your subject, pull out the bung, and let nature caper."

The Bible is " the Sword of the Spirit." The problem is how to wield it; how to make use of the knowledge we have of it. There are some who mount the pulpit, and, fleet of foot like Ahimaaz, they outstrip the slower but better informed Cushis, and obtain earlier audience of the king, but they have no tidings ready, and when called upon to speak they have nothing to say (2 Sam. 18:19-33). " Get full of your subject." Master the content of. the Word of God. Illustrations and divisions, exordiums and perorations, grammar and rhetoric will then take care of themselves.

The man who knows his Bible, and knows it to some purpose, will first of all apply its truths to his own personal conduct and daily life. And he will find it all that David, in the 119th Psalm, declares it to be : a source,of blessing, a defence against iniquity, a fountain of honour, a vision of wonder, a loosening of. the tongue, an enlarging of the heart, a source of comfort and quickening, of establishment and salvation. When David meditated in the law of the Lord, he began to talk, he began to sing, he began to run, he was wiser than his enemies, he knew more than his teachers, he opened his mouth and panted, he rose early before the dawn that he might meditate in the Word, and said of its testimonies, "I love them exceedingly." That is the universal experience and the universal testimony of all those who make themselves acquainted with the love-kindling, life-quickening properties of the Word of God.

The ultimate. reality of our life is the life we live with God. The way to live with God is the way of intimate knowledge of His holy will, through loving obedience to His holy Word.

It is one of the unfailing characteristics of those who obtain an intimate knowledge of the Word of God, that their hearts immediately begin to burn with the desire to communicate that knowledge to others. They have " something to say." They are "full of it." They are possessed by it. They have only to " pull out the bung " and nature will immediately begin to " caper."

This fulness of knowledge finds appropriate utterance on the most unlikely occasions. It is never out of place. It never gives offence. The business of the Christian minister, the lay- preacher, the Sunday School teacher, the city missionary, the Church member, is by sermon, by lesson, by conversation, by example, to wield "the Sword of the Spirit which is the Word of God." But the Word must be read, and studied, and believed ; it must be loved, and honoured, and obeyed, in order that it may be to others in like manner their joy and their salvation.

Chapter 7
How to Enthrone the Bible

THE Bible is the word of a King. We must give it its rightful place. It was not given to be criticised. It was given to be obeyed. The Church is its custodian, not its creator. Reason is its offspring, not its judge. Man cannot investigate God. The knowledge of things we can take ; the knowledge of God, God must give. All we can do is to accept the revelation given and say, "Speak, Lord, for thy servant heareth " (I Sam.3:9). The organ by which we, obtain the knowledge of God is that revelation of Himself which He has given us in the Bible. " Behold I have taught you statutes and judgments, even as the Lord my God commanded me. Keep therefore and do them ; for this is your wisdom and your understanding in the sight of the nations. . . . For what nation is there so great, who hath God so nigh unto them, as the Lord our God is in all things that we call upon him for? And what nation is there so great, that hath statutes and judgments so righteous as all this law, which I set before you this day?" (Deut.4:6-8). "The fear of the Lord, that is wisdom ; and to depart from evil is understanding" (Job. 28:28). " The fear of the Lord is the beginning of wisdom : a good understanding have all they that do his commandments" (Ps. 111:10). Man cannot as critic place himself above God. The object God-excludes all idea of co-ordination and comparison. Faith in Holy Scripture is an indispensable pre-requisite in the search for truth when the search relates to the knowledge of God. " Canst thou by searching find out God? Canst thou find out the Almighty unto perfection?" (Job 11: 7). " O the depth of the riches both of the wisdom and knowledge of God ! How unsearchable are his judgments, and his. ways past finding out! " (Rom. 11: 33).

Such knowledge is too wonderful for me; it is high, I cannot attain unto it " (Ps. 139: 6). " O Lord thou hast searched me and known me " (Ps. 139:1), but I cannot search and know Thee, except as I "search the Scriptures " in which The hast revealed Thyself to me. God is never a passive phenomenon. All our knowledge of God is the fruit of His activity in revealing Himself to us, and this knowledge can only come to us from the living God Himself, and through Holy Scripture, in which it lies open to all who are willing to receive it. Those who have no faith in Holy Scripture can never attain to the, knowledge of God, for there is no other organ except faith and no other vehicle except revelation through which the knowledge of God can reach us.

Man is an abnormal being, a fallen creature. Apart from regeneration he cannot investigate and criticise and pass judgment upon Holy Scripture. His darkened understanding cannot discriminate between what is true and what is false in the revelation which God has given us of Himself. Regeneration alone annuls and conquers sin and restores to perverted human nature its original capacity for knowing God, and regeneration is always through the Word. Those who place reason above revelation presume that they have by nature a faculty for judging the Word of God which only the Word of God can create.

Holy Scripture is the rock-bottom fact of our religious life. It does not rest on any deeper fact more fundamental than itself. The sense of sin does not come to us by nature. It is not awakened in us by reflection. It is not generated in us by the exercise of reason. It is quickened in us by the Word of God. Revelation restores the organ of the knowledge of God for which reason, apart from revelation, is no substitute. Revelation is the basis of reason,and by revelation reason is restored to its rightful place in the happy ordering and good government of the powers of the soul. It is the function of reason to complete the fabric, the foundations of which are laid in revelation. It is the function of revelation to lay the foundations upon which reason shall erect the superstructure of the knowledge of God.

The organ of the knowledge of God is revelation, i.e. Holy Scripture. Holy Scripture is a transcript of the mind of God. God does not impart the knowledge of Himself directly and immediately to each individual afresh. He makes Himself known to us once for all in Holy Scripture. The faith, the thing to be believed, " the faith which was once for all delivered unto the saints " (Jude 1:3) is the whole extent and content of Holy Scripture. Nothing can be added to it. Nothing can be taken from it. Nothing can be altered in it. It has been placed in the custody of the saints, not in the custody of unbelieving scholars, whose knowledge of Hebrew and Greek is no substitute for the experience of regeneration. No amount of scholarship will qualify an unregenerate man to understand the Bible, much less to teach it.

The knowledge of God imparted in Scripture is an organic whole. There is one central revelation for all, not a separate revelation for each. The revelation is not continuous. It is not repeated. There is such a thing as present-day illumination, for illumination is the present-day work of the Holy Spirit. in appropriating Holy Scripture, and applying it to the hearts of men ; but there is no such thing as present-day inspiration, for inspiration is the process of which revelation, i.e. Holy Scripture, is the result, and the revelation is complete. The thing is done.

The finished product lies before us in the compact volume of the sixty-six books of the Bible. Inspiration is the activity of God in the mind of the prophets who wrote the Old Testament, and the apostles who wrote the New Testament. Inspiration is over. It is a thing accomplished. If inspiration were continuous, the result of it would be the continuous production of other works of the same rank and quality as the books of the Bible. Inspiration is designed to restore the knowledge of God which reason does not and cannot give.

The revelation of the knowledge of God is not given to us in the Bible. It is the Bible. The Bible is the Word of God, not contains it. The Bible is not a conglomerate of different elements partly human and partly Divine. It is pure gold. We have no natural endowment by the exercise of which we can pronounce judgment on the truth of the Word of God. We must pass the modern mind through the crucible of the Word of God, not the Word of God through the, crucible of the modern mind. The form and content of the Word are organically one. The Church is the custodian, not the creator, not the critic, and not the judge of the Word. Under the providence of God the task of preserving ,the true Text and the exact content of the Word has been faithfully fulfilled. The errors of copyists are easily detected. The true readings are easily restored. The Text is not open to alteration, emendation, or amendment with a view to its being brought into harmony with the latest phase of modern thought. We must judge the opinions of men by the Word, not the Word by the opinions of men. The limits of the Word are strictly defined and for ever sure. They are those of the whole Bible, not merely those of the Bible as a whole. Ice and cold are organically one. Melt the ice and the cold disappears. Alter the form of Scripture, attempt to separate the dross from the pure, the human element from the Divine, and the sure content of the Word is gone and with it all true knowledge of God. We must hold for truth all that God has revealed as truth in His Word. The eternal need, the urgent need, the pressing need of the age in which we live, is the need of the enthronement of the Bible in the heart and conscience, the affection and the will of the people of God and the nations of the world. We enthrone the Word when we read and ponder, when we love and reverence, when we practise and obey, when we proclaim and magnify the saving truths which it enshrines, and the holy precepts which it enjoins.

The moment we open the Word of God, that moment God presents Himself before us. He comes in it and by it into our very soul. Holy Scripture is never something near from a God afar off. It brings God near. It is God near. The word of God is alive. It is His voice. God Himself bears witness to its truth. It cannot be made more sure. It cannot be otherwise made known. All faith in God is quickened by Scripture. All faith in Scripture is quickened by God, and is invincible. There is no need and no room for further proof, or demonstration, or support from observation, experience or reason. Faith gives us the highest possible assurance. The supremacy of the Word is guaranteed by the immediate testimony of the Spirit of God.

Chapter 8
How to Defend the Bible

THE best way to defend a lion, shut up in a cage, is to let him out of it. He will then speedily devise ample and majestic means to defend himself. The best way to defend the Bible is to expound it. If ' you want to understand the Bible, read it. If you want to enjoy the Bible, read it. If you want to authenticate the Bible, read it. If you want to study the Bible, take pains with it. If you want to master the Bible, wrestle with it. If you want to wield the Bible, get possession of it. If you want to enthrone the Bible, get possessed by it. If you want to defend the Bible, let it speak for itself.

This does not mean that there is any weakness in the arguments which prove the truth of its astounding claims. On the contrary every attack upon the genuineness- and the authenticity of the various books, the integrity and the purity of the Text, and the Divine authority of the Canon, has been triumphantly repelled.

The science of Textual Criticism has amply vindicated the claim that the Bible, as it was held in the hands of our Lord, is the Bible as we hold it in our hands to-day. The "assured results" of the " Higher Criticism," reversing the traditional view of the date, authorship, and composition of the books of the Bible, and unduly emphasising the so-called "human element" in Scripture at the expense of the so-called " Divine element " in it, have been examined in detail and have been proved to be entirely dependent upon naturalistic assumptions and speculative presuppositions that would not be entertained for a moment by any person capable of pronouncing judgment upon evidence brought forward in a court of law ; whilst the vagaries of " Historical Criticism " have reached their climax and their reductio ad absurdum in the doubts now beginning to be entertained as to the historical character of the events of the life of our Lord, the surest and best-attested events in human history.

The critics have been refuted, and the Bible has been vindicated, but still the controversy goes on. The Book has always had its enemies. It has always been attacked. Christianity itself has always been opposed from the very first. The best defence of Christianity is not a clever argument, which can always be met by a cleverer one, but the life of a truly noble Christian man and in which its high principles are adequately realised and faithfully expressed, and the best defence of the Bible is the life of a truly devout, Bible student in which its holy precepts are lovingly enshrined.

www.ingramcontent.com/pod-product-compliance
Lightning Source LLC
Chambersburg PA
CBHW032014040426
42448CB00006B/623